MW01608868

Rethinking Education

Towards a global common good?

Published in 2015 by the United Nations Educational, Scientific and Cultural Organization,
7, place de Fontenoy, 75352 Paris 07 SP, France

© UNESCO 2015

ISBN 978-92-3-100088-1

This publication is available in Open Access under the Attribution-ShareAlike 3.0 IGO (CC-BY-SA 3.0 IGO) license
(http://creativecommons.org/licenses/by-sa/3.0/igo/). By using the content of this publication, the users accept
to be bound by the terms of use of the UNESCO Open Access Repository (http://www.unesco.org/open-access/
terms-use-ccbysa-en).

The designations employed and the presentation of material throughout this publication do not imply the expression of
any opinion whatsoever on the part of UNESCO concerning the legal status of any country, territory, city or area or
of its authorities, or concerning the delimitation of its frontiers or boundaries.

The members of the Senior Experts' Group are responsible for the choice and the presentation of the facts contained
in the publication and for the opinions expressed therein. These are not necessarily those of UNESCO and do not
commit the Organization.

Graphic design: UNESCO

Cover photo credit: © Shutterstock / Arthimedes

Printed by UNESCO

Printed in France

Foreword

What education do we need for the 21st century? What is the purpose of education in the current context of societal transformation? How should learning be organized? These questions inspired the ideas presented in this publication.

In the spirit of two landmark UNESCO publications, *Learning to Be: The world of education today and tomorrow* (1972), the 'Faure Report', and *Learning: The treasure within* (1996), the 'Delors Report', I am convinced we need to think big again today about education.

For these are turbulent times. The world is getting younger, and aspirations for human rights and dignity are rising. Societies are more connected than ever, but intolerance and conflict remain rife. New power hubs are emerging, but inequalities are deepening and the planet is under pressure. Opportunities for sustainable and inclusive development are vast, but challenges are steep and complex.

The world is changing – education must also change. Societies everywhere are undergoing deep transformation, and this calls for new forms of education to foster the competencies that societies and economies need, today and tomorrow. This means moving beyond literacy and numeracy, to focus on learning environments and on new approaches to learning for greater justice, social equity and global solidarity. Education must be about learning to live on a planet under pressure. It must be about cultural literacy, on the basis of respect and equal dignity, helping to weave together the social, economic and environmental dimensions of sustainable development.

This is a humanist vision of education as an essential common good. I believe this vision renews with the inspiration of the UNESCO Constitution, agreed 70 years ago, while reflecting new times and demands.

Education is key to the global integrated framework of sustainable development goals. Education is at the heart of our efforts both to adapt to change and to transform the world within which we live. A quality basic education is the necessary foundation for learning throughout life in a complex and rapidly changing world.

Across the world, we have seen great progress in expanding learning opportunities for all. Yet we must draw the right lessons to chart a new course forward. Access is not enough; we need a new focus on the quality of education and the relevance of learning, on what children, youth and adults are actually learning. Schooling and formal education are essential, but we must widen the angle, to foster learning throughout life. Getting girls into primary school is vital, but we must help them all the way through secondary and beyond. We need an ever stronger focus on teachers and educators as change agents across the board.

There is no more powerful transformative force than education – to promote human rights and dignity, to eradicate poverty and deepen sustainability, to build a better future for all, founded on equal rights and social justice, respect for cultural diversity, and international solidarity and shared responsibility, all of which are fundamental aspects of our common humanity.

This is why we must think big again and re-vision education in a changing world. For this, we need debate and dialogue across the board, and that is the goal of this publication – to be both aspirational and inspirational, to speak to new times.

Irina Bokova
Director-General of UNESCO

Acknowledgements

I am pleased to see this publication released at this particular historical juncture when the international education and development community moves towards the global framework of Sustainable Development Goals. The present publication is the result of my early discussions with Ms Irina Bokova, Director-General of UNESCO, during her first mandate. She strongly supported the idea of reviewing the 'Delors Report' in order to identify future orientations of global education. She wisely wished to demonstrate that, beyond its lead technical role in the Education for All movement, UNESCO also has an important intellectual leadership role in international education.

It is in this perspective that the Director-General of UNESCO established a Senior Experts' Group to rethink education in a changing world. The group of international experts was tasked with preparing a succinct document that identified issues likely to affect the organization of learning and to stimulate debate on a vision for education. The group was co-chaired by Ms Amina J. Mohammed, Special Advisor to the United Nations Secretary-General on Post-2015 Development Planning and Assistant Secretary-General, and Professor W. John Morgan, UNESCO Chair at the University of Nottingham, in the United Kingdom. Other members of the Senior Experts' Group included: Mr Peter Ronald DeSouza, Professor at the Centre for the Study of Developing Societies, New Delhi, India; Mr Georges Haddad, Professor at Université Paris 1 Panthéon-Sorbonne, France; Ms Fadia Kiwan, Director Emeritus of the Institut des Sciences Politiques at Université Saint-Joseph in Beirut, Lebanon; Mr Fred van Leeuwen, Secretary-General of Education International; Mr Teiichi Sato, Professor at the International University of Health and Welfare in Japan; and Ms Sylvia Schmelkes, President of the National Institute for the Evaluation of Education in Mexico.

From the outset, the Director-General gave the UNESCO Education Sector strong support to undertake this project. Coordinated by the Education Research and Foresight team, the Group met in Paris in February 2013, February 2014, and December 2014 to develop their ideas and debate successive drafts of their text. I would like to take this opportunity to sincerely thank all the members of the Senior Experts' Group for their invaluable contribution to this important collective endeavour. The UNESCO Education Sector is very grateful for their efforts and commitment.

This publication would not have been possible without the contribution of numerous people, external experts as well as UNESCO colleagues. I would like to acknowledge and thank them for their support: Abdeljalil Akkari (University of Geneva), Massimo Amadio (UNESCO International Bureau of Education), David Atchoarena (UNESCO Division for Policies and Lifelong Learning Systems), Sylvain Aubry (Global Initiative for Economic, Social and Cultural Rights), Néjib Ayed (Arab League Educational, Cultural and Scientific Organization), Aaron Benavot (Education for All Global Monitoring Report), Mark Bray (University of Hong Kong), Arne Carlsen (UNESCO Institute for Lifelong Learning), Michel Carton (Network of International Policies and Cooperation in Education and Training), Borhene Chakroun (UNESCO Section for Youth, Literacy and Skills Development), Kai-ming Cheng (University of Hong Kong), Maren Elfert (University of British Columbia), Paulin J. Hountondji (National Council of Education of Benin), Klaus Hüfner (Freie Universität Berlin), Ruth Kagia (Results for Development), Taeyoung Kang (POSCO Research Institute, Seoul), Maria Khan (Asia South Pacific Association for Basic and Adult Education), Valérie Leichti (Swiss Agency for Development Cooperation), Candy Lugas (UNESCO International Institute for Educational Planning), Ian Macpherson (Open Society Foundations), Rolla Moumne Beulque (UNESCO Section of Education Policy), Renato Opertti (UNESCO International Bureau of Education), Svein Osttveit (Executive Office, UNESCO Education Sector), David Post (Education for All Global Monitoring Report), Sheldon Shaeffer (Specialist on Early Childhood Education and Governance), Dennis Sinyolo (Education International), and Rosa-Maria Torres (Instituto Fronesis, Quito).

Finally, I am grateful to the Education Research and Foresight team at UNESCO for bringing this project to fruition. Initiated by Georges Haddad, former Director of the team, the drafting process was led and coordinated by Sobhi Tawil, Senior Programme Specialist. They were assisted by Rita Locatelli and Luca Solesin from the UNESCO Chair on Human Rights and Ethics of International Cooperation at the University of Bergamo, Italy, as well as by Huong Le Thu, Programme Specialist at UNESCO. Other research assistants included Marie Cougoureux, Jiawen Li, Giorgiana Maciuca, Guillermo Nino Valdehita, Victor Nouis, Marion Poutrel, Hélène Verrue and Shan Yin.

Qian Tang, Ph.D.
Assistant Director-General for Education

Contents

List of boxes

Executive summary

The changes in the world today are characterized by new levels of complexity and contradiction. These changes generate tensions for which education is expected to prepare individuals and communities by giving them the capability to adapt and to respond. This publication contributes to rethinking education and learning in this context. It builds on one of UNESCO's main tasks as a global observatory of social transformation with the objective of stimulating public policy debate.

It is a call for dialogue among all stakeholders. It is inspired by a humanistic vision of education and development, based on respect for life and human dignity, equal rights, social justice, cultural diversity, international solidarity, and shared responsibility for a sustainable future. These are the fundamentals of our common humanity. This book enhances the vision provided by the two landmark UNESCO publications: *Learning to Be: The world of education today and tomorrow* (1972), the 'Faure Report', and *Learning: The treasure within* (1996), the 'Delors Report'.

Sustainable development: A central concern

The aspiration of sustainable development requires us to resolve common problems and tensions and to recognize new horizons. Economic growth and the creation of wealth have reduced global poverty rates, but vulnerability, inequality, exclusion and violence have increased within and across societies throughout the world. Unsustainable patterns of economic production and consumption contribute to global warming, environmental degradation and an upsurge in natural disasters. Moreover, while international human rights frameworks have been strengthened over the past several decades, the implementation and protection of these norms remain a challenge. For example, despite the progressive empowerment of women through greater access to education, they continue to face discrimination in public life and in employment. Violence against women and children, particularly girls, continues to undermine their rights. Again, while technological development contributes to greater interconnectedness and offers new avenues for exchange, cooperation and solidarity, we also see an increase in cultural and religious intolerance, identity-based political mobilization and conflict.

Education must find ways of responding to such challenges, taking into account multiple worldviews and alternative knowledge systems, as well as new frontiers in science and technology such as the advances in neurosciences and the developments in digital technology. Rethinking the purpose of education and the organization of learning has never been more urgent.

Reaffirming a humanistic approach to education

Education alone cannot hope to solve all development challenges, but a humanistic and holistic approach to education can and should contribute to achieving a new development model. In such a model, economic growth must be guided by environmental stewardship and by concern for peace, inclusion and social justice. The ethical and moral principles of a humanistic approach to development stand against violence, intolerance, discrimination and exclusion. Regarding education and learning, it means going beyond narrow utilitarianism and economism to integrate the multiple dimensions of human existence. This approach emphasizes the inclusion of people who are often subject to discrimination – women and girls, indigenous people, persons with disabilities, migrants, the elderly and people living in countries affected by conflict. It requires an open and flexible approach to learning that is both lifelong and life-wide: an approach that provides the opportunity for all to realize their potential for a sustainable future and a life of dignity. This humanistic approach has implications for the definition of learning content and pedagogies, as well as for the role of teachers and other educators. It is even more relevant given the rapid development of new technologies, in particular digital technologies.

Local and global policy-making in a complex world

The escalating levels of social and economic complexity present a number of challenges for education policy-making in today's globalized world. The intensification of economic globalization is producing patterns of low-employment growth, rising youth unemployment and vulnerable employment. While the trends point to a growing disconnection between education and the fast-changing world of work, they also represent an opportunity to reconsider the link between education and societal development. Furthermore, the increasing mobility of learners and workers across national borders and the new patterns of knowledge and skills transfer require new ways of recognizing, validating and assessing learning. Regarding citizenship, the challenge for national education systems is to shape identities, and to promote awareness of and a sense of responsibility for others in an increasingly interconnected and interdependent world.

The expansion of access to education worldwide over the past several decades is placing greater pressure on public financing. Additionally, the demand has grown in recent years for voice in public affairs and for the involvement of non-state actors in education, at both national and global levels. This diversification of partnerships is blurring the boundaries between public and private, posing problems for the democratic governance of education. In short, there is a growing need to reconcile the contributions and demands of the three regulators of social behaviour: society, state and market.

Recontextualizing education and knowledge as global common goods

In light of this rapidly changing reality, we need to rethink the normative principles that guide educational governance: in particular, the right to education and the notion of education as a public good. Indeed, we often refer to education as a human right and as a public good in international education discourse. Yet, while these principles are relatively uncontested at the level of basic education, there is no general agreement, in much of the discussion, about their applicability to post-basic education and training. To what extent does the right to education, and the principle of public good, apply also to non-formal and informal education, which are less institutionalized, if at all? Therefore a concern for knowledge – understood as the information, understanding, skills, values and attitudes acquired through learning – is central to any discussion of the purpose of education.

The authors propose that both knowledge and education be considered *common goods*. This implies that the creation of knowledge, as well as its acquisition, validation and use, are common to all people as part of a *collective societal endeavour*. The notion of common good allows us to go beyond the influence of an individualistic socio-economic theory inherent to the notion of 'public good'. It emphasizes a participatory process in defining what is a common good, which takes into account a diversity of contexts, concepts of well-being and knowledge ecosystems. Knowledge is an inherent part of the common heritage of humanity. Given the need for sustainable development in an increasingly interdependent world, education and knowledge should, therefore, be considered *global common goods*. Inspired by the value of solidarity grounded in our common humanity, the principle of knowledge and education as global common goods has implications for the roles and responsibilities of the diverse stakeholders. This holds true for international organizations such as UNESCO, which has a global observatory and normative function qualifying it to promote and guide global public policy debate.

Considerations for the future

As we attempt to reconcile the purpose and organization of learning as a collective societal endeavour, the following questions may serve as first steps towards debate: While the four pillars of learning – to know, to do, to be, and to live together – are still relevant, they are threatened by globalization and by the resurgence of identity politics. How can they be strengthened and renewed? How can education respond to the challenges of achieving economic, social and environmental sustainability? How can a plurality of worldviews be reconciled through a humanistic approach to education? How can such a humanistic approach be realized through educational policies and practices? What are the implications of globalization for national policies and decision-making in education? How should education be financed? What are the specific implications for teacher education, training, development and support? What are the implications for education of the distinction between the concepts of the private good, the public good, and the common good?

Diverse stakeholders with their multiple perspectives should be brought together to share research findings and to articulate normative principles in the guidance of policy. UNESCO, as an intellectual agency and think tank, can provide the platform for such debate and dialogue, enhancing our understanding of new approaches to education policy and provision, with the aim of sustaining humanity and its common well-being.

Introduction

Introduction

❝Education breeds confidence. Confidence breeds hope. Hope breeds peace.❞

Confucius, Chinese philosopher (551-479 BC)

A call for dialogue

This is a contribution to re-visioning education in a changing world and builds on one of UNESCO's main tasks as a global observatory of social transformation. Its purpose is to stimulate public policy debate focused specifically on education in a changing world. It is a *call for dialogue* inspired by a humanistic vision of education and development based on principles of *respect for life and human dignity*, *equal rights and social justice*, *respect for cultural diversity*, and *international solidarity and shared responsibility*, all of which are fundamental aspects of our *common humanity*. It is intended to be both aspirational and inspirational, speaking to new times and to everyone across the world with a stake in education. It is written in the spirit of the two landmark UNESCO publications: *Learning to Be: The world of education today and tomorrow*, the 1972 'Faure Report'; and *Learning: The treasure within*, the 1996 'Delors Report'.

Looking back to see ahead[1]

In re-visioning education and learning for the future, we must build upon the legacy of past analyses. The 1972 Faure Report, for instance, established the two interrelated notions of the *learning society* and *lifelong education* at a time when traditional education systems were being challenged. As technological progress and social change accelerated, the report said, no one could expect that a person's initial education would serve them throughout their life. School, while remaining the essential means

---

[1] Adapted from Morgan, W. J. and White, I. 2013. Looking backward to see ahead: The Faure and Delors reports and the post-2015 development agenda. *Zeitschrift Weiterbildung*, No. 4, pp. 40-43.

Rethinking Education • Towards a global common good?

for transmitting organized knowledge, would be supplemented by other aspects of social life – social institutions, the work environment, leisure, the media. The report advocated the right and necessity of each individual to learn for their own personal, social, economic, political and cultural development. It affirmed lifelong education as the keystone of educational policies in both developing and developed countries.[2]

The 1996 Delors Report proposed an integrated vision of education based on two key concepts, 'learning throughout life' and the four pillars of learning, to know, to do, to live together, and to be. It was not in itself a blueprint for educational reform, but rather a basis for reflection and debate about what choices should be made in formulating policies. The report argued that choices about education were determined by choices about what kind of society we wished to live in. Beyond education's immediate functionality, it considered the formation of the whole person to be an essential part of education's purpose.[3] The Delors Report was aligned closely with the moral and intellectual principles that underpin UNESCO, and therefore its analysis and recommendations were more humanistic and less instrumental and market-driven than other education reform studies of the time.[4]

The Faure and Delors reports have undoubtedly inspired education policy worldwide,[5] but now we must recognize that the global context has undergone significant transformation in its intellectual and material landscape since the 1970s and again since the 1990s. This second decade of the twenty-first century marks a new historical juncture, bringing with it different challenges and fresh opportunities for human learning and development. We are entering a new historical phase characterized by the interconnectedness and interdependency of societies and by new levels of complexity, uncertainty and tensions.

An emerging global context for learning

The situation around the world today is characterized by a number of paradoxes. While the intensification of economic globalization has reduced global poverty, it is also producing patterns of low-employment growth, rising youth unemployment and vulnerable employment. Economic globalization is also widening inequalities, between and within countries. Educational systems contribute to these inequalities by ignoring the educational needs of students in disadvantage and of many living in poor countries, while at the same time concentrating educational opportunities among the affluent, thus making high-quality training and education very exclusive. Current patterns of economic growth, coupled with demographic growth and urbanization, are depleting

2   Medel-Añonuevo, C., Oshako, T. and Mauch, W. 2001. *Revisiting lifelong learning for the 21st century.* Hamburg, UNESCO Institute for Education.
3   Power, C. N. 1997. Learning: a means or an end? A look at the Delors Report and its implications for educational renewal. *Prospects,* Vol. XXVII, No. 2, p.118.
4   Ibid.
5   For a discussion of this see, for example, Tawil, S. and Cougoureux, M. 2013. *Revisiting Learning: The treasure within – Assessing the influence of the 1996 Delors report.* Paris, UNESCO Education Research and Foresight, ERF Occasional Papers, No. 4; Elfert, M. 2015. UNESCO, the Faure report, the Delors report, and the political utopia of lifelong learning. *European Journal of Education,* 50.1, pp. 88-100.

non-renewable natural resources and polluting the environment, causing irreversible ecological damage and climate change. Furthermore, along with growing recognition of cultural diversity (whether historically inherent to nation-states or resulting from greater migration and mobility), we also note a dramatic increase in cultural and religious chauvinism and in identity-based political mobilization and violence. Terrorism, drug-related violence, wars and internal conflicts and even intra-family and school-related violence are mounting. These patterns of violence raise questions for education in its capacity to shape values and attitudes for living together. Additionally, as a result of such conflicts and crises, almost 30 million children are deprived of their right to a basic education, creating generations of uneducated future adults who are too often ignored in development policies. These issues are fundamental challenges for human understanding of others and for social cohesion across the globe.

At the same time, we are witnessing a greater demand for *voice* in public affairs in a changing context of local and global governance. The spectacular progress in internet connectivity, mobile technologies and other digital media, combined with the democratization of access to public education and the development of different forms of private education, is transforming patterns of social, civic and political engagement. Additionally, the greater mobility of workers and learners between countries, across jobs and in learning spaces intensifies the need to reconsider how learning and competencies are recognized, validated and assessed.

The changes taking place have implications for education and signal the emergence of a new global context for learning. Not all of these changes call for educational policy responses, but in any case they are forging new conditions. They require not only new practices, but also new perspectives from which to understand the nature of learning and the role of knowledge and education in human development. This new context of societal transformation demands that we revisit the purpose of education and the organization of learning.

What is meant by knowledge, learning and education?

Knowledge is central to any discussion of learning and may be understood as the way in which individuals and societies apply meaning to experience. It can therefore be seen broadly as the information, understanding, skills, values and attitudes acquired through learning. As such, knowledge is linked inextricably to the cultural, social, environmental and institutional contexts in which it is created and reproduced.[6]

Learning is understood here to be the process of acquiring such knowledge. It is both a *process* and the *result* of that process; a means, as well as an end; an individual practice as well as a collective endeavour. Learning is a multifaceted reality defined by the context. What knowledge is acquired and why, where, when and how it is used

---

6   European Science Foundation. 2011. *Responses to Environmental and Societal Challenges for our Unstable Earth (RESCUE). ESF Forward Look – ESF-COST 'Frontier of Science' joint initiative.* Strasbourg/ Brussels, European Science Foundation/European Cooperation in Science and Technology.

represent fundamental questions for the development of individuals and societies alike.

Education is understood here to mean learning that is deliberate, intentional, purposeful and organized. Formal and non-formal educational opportunities suppose a certain degree of institutionalization. A great deal of learning, however, is much less institutionalized, if at all, even when it is intentional and deliberate. Such informal education, less organized and structured than either formal or non-formal education, may include learning activities that occur in the work place (for instance, internships), in the local community and in daily life, on a self-directed, family-directed, or socially-directed basis.[7]

Finally, it is important to note that much of what we learn in life is neither deliberate nor intentional. This informal learning is inherent to all experiences of socialization. The discussion that follows, however, is restricted to learning that is intentional and organized.

> What knowledge is acquired and why, where, when and how it is used represent fundamental questions for the development of individuals and societies alike.

Organization of the publication

Inspired by a central concern for sustainable human and social development, the first section outlines some of the trends, tensions and contradictions in today's process of global social transformation, as well as the new knowledge horizons that it offers. At the same time, the section highlights the need to explore alternative approaches to human well-being, including an acknowledgement of the diversity of worldviews and knowledge systems, and the need to sustain them.

The second section reaffirms a humanistic approach, stressing the need for an integrated approach to education based on renewed ethical and moral foundations. It calls for an education process that is inclusive and does not simply reproduce inequalities. In the changing global landscape of education, the role of teachers and other educators is vital for developing critical thinking and independent judgement, rather than unreflective conformity.

The next section examines issues linked to educational policy-making in a complex world. These include the challenges of recognizing and responding to the gap between formal education and employment; of recognizing and validating learning in a world of increasing mobility across borders, professional occupations and learning spaces; and of rethinking citizenship education in an increasingly globalized world, balancing respect for plurality with the universal values and concern for our common humanity. Finally, we consider the complexities of national policy-making in education in the context of potential forms of global governance.

---

[7]   Ibid.

The fourth section explores the need to recontextualize foundational principles for the governance of education, particularly the right to education and the principle of education as a public good. It proposes that greater attention be paid in education policy to knowledge, and to the ways in which it is created, accessed, acquired, validated and used. It also suggests the need to recontextualize the foundational principles that govern the organization of education, in particular the principle of education as a *public good*. It proposes that considering education and knowledge to be *global common goods* might provide a useful way to reconcile the purpose and organization of learning as a collective societal endeavour in a changing world. The concluding section sums up the key ideas and puts forward questions for further debate.

1. Sustainable development:
A central concern

1. Sustainable development: A central concern

"We ought to think that we are one of the leaves of a tree, and the tree is all of humanity. We cannot live without others, without the tree."

Pablo Casals, Spanish cellist and conductor

In revisiting the purpose of education, our vision is guided by a central concern for sustainable human and social development. Sustainability is understood as the responsible action of individuals and societies towards a better future for all, locally and globally – one in which social justice and environmental stewardship guide socio-economic development. The changes in today's interconnected and interdependent world are bringing new levels of complexity, tensions and paradoxes, as well as new knowledge horizons that we need to consider. Such patterns of change require efforts to explore alternative approaches to progress and to human well-being.

■ Challenges and tensions

The Delors Report identified a number of tensions generated by technological, economic and social change. They included tensions between the global and the local; the universal and the particular; tradition and modernity; the spiritual and the material; long term and short term considerations; the need for competition and the ideal of equality of opportunity; and the expansion of knowledge and our capacity to assimilate it. These seven tensions remain useful perspectives from which to view the current dynamics of social transformation. Some are taking on new meaning, with fresh tensions emerging. These include patterns of economic growth characterized by rising vulnerability, growing inequality, increased ecological stress, and rising intolerance and violence. Finally, while there has been progress in human rights, implementation of norms often remains a challenge.

Ecological stress and unsustainable patterns of economic production and consumption

Ensuring growth has long been understood as the purpose of development, based on the premise that economic growth generates positive effects that eventually guarantee greater well-being for all. However, unsustainable patterns of production and consumption point to fundamental contradictions in a dominant model of development focused on economic growth. As a consequence of unhindered growth and overexploitation of natural areas, climate change is producing an increase in natural disasters, putting poor countries particularly at great risk. Indeed, sustainability has emerged as a central development concern in the face of climate change, the degradation of vital natural resources such as water, and the loss of biodiversity.

> The changes in today's interconnected and interdependent world are bringing new levels of complexity, tensions and paradoxes, as well as new knowledge horizons that we need to consider.

In the latter part of the twentieth century (1960-2000), water use doubled, food consumption and production increased 2.5 times and wood consumption tripled. The upsurge was driven by demographic growth. The world population almost tripled in the second half of the twentieth century, growing from some 2.5 billion in 1950 to over 7 billion in 2013, and it is expected to climb to over 8 billion in 2025.[8] It is estimated that by 2030, demand for food will rise at least 35 per cent, demand for water by 40 per cent, and demand for energy by 50 per cent.[9]

Moreover, for the first time, more than half of the world's population lives in urban areas. By 2050, two-thirds of the world population, or over 6 billion persons, will do so.[10] By then, it is estimated that 80 per cent of the urban population of the world will be concentrated in cities and towns of the global South.[11] The growth of the world's urban population, combined with the expansion of middle class lifestyles and patterns of consumption and production, are having an adverse impact on the environment and on climate change, and increasing the risk of natural disasters worldwide.[12] These

---

[8]   UN DESA. 2013. *World Population Prospects: The 2012 Revision.* New York, United Nations. Most of this growth has taken place and will continue to take place in the global South. The share of the total world population in the global South grew from 66% in 1950 to 82% in 2010. This amount is expected to further increase to 86% by 2050 and to 88% by 2100.

[9]   National Intelligence Council. 2012. *Global Trends 2030: Alternative worlds.* Washington, DC, National Intelligence Council.

[10]   UN DESA. 2012. *World Urbanization Prospects: The 2011 Revision.* New York, United Nations.

[11]   UN-HABITAT. 2013. *UN-HABITAT Global Activities Report 2013. Our presence and partnerships.* Nairobi, UN-HABITAT.

[12]   SPREAD Sustainable Lifestyle 2050. 2011. *Sustainable Lifestyle: Today's facts and Tomorrow's trends.* Amsterdam, SPREAD Sustainable Lifestyle 2050.

upheavals pose a fundamental threat to lives, livelihoods and public health across the world. Unplanned or poorly planned urbanization is increasingly vulnerable to natural disasters and extreme climate conditions. The unprecedented rate of urban growth is setting the social, political, cultural and environmental trends of the world. Consequently, sustainable urbanization has become one of the most pressing challenges facing the global community in the twenty-first century.[13]

These patterns of demographic growth and urbanization also have important implications for the institutional arrangements and partnerships required to ensure the provision of relevant and flexible educational opportunities from a lifelong learning perspective. The proportion of the elderly in the overall population is projected to double by 2050,[14] together with greater demand for more diversified adult education and training. Ensuring the projected increase in the working age population in Africa translates into a demographic dividend[15] will require the provision of relevant education and training opportunities throughout life.

Greater wealth but rising vulnerability and growing inequalities

Global rates of poverty declined by half between 1990 and 2010. This decline in poverty is largely a result of robust rates of economic growth observed in emerging economies, as well as in many countries in Africa, and this despite the global financial and economic crisis of 2008. It is expected that the middle classes in the developing world will continue to expand substantially over the next fifteen to twenty years, with some of the most rapid growth taking place in China and in India.[16] However, significant disparities persist across the world and poverty rates vary considerably among the diverse regions of the world.[17]

Patterns of strong gross domestic product (GDP) growth are not always generating the levels of employment required, nor the type of jobs desired. Employment opportunities are not expanding sufficiently to keep up with the growing labour force. Over 200 million people were unemployed in 2013 around the world, and global unemployment is set to increase further. The regions that have experienced the bulk of the increase in global unemployment such as East Asia, South Asia and Sub-Saharan Africa have also experienced declining job quality. Vulnerable employment accounts currently for almost half of total employment and has contributed to the number of workers living below or very near the poverty line. Persons in vulnerable employment are much more

---

13 United Nations Human Settlement Programme, UN-Habitat, www.un-ngls.org/spip.php?page=article_fr_s&id_article=819 [Accessed February 2015].

14 UN DESA. 2013. *World Population Prospects: The 2012 Revision.* New York, United Nations.

15 Drummond, P., Thakoor, V. and Yu, S. 2014. *Africa Rising: Harnessing the Demographic Dividend.* IMF Working Paper 14/43. International Monetary Fund.

16 National Intelligence Council. 2012. *Global Trends 2030: Alternative worlds.* Washington, DC, National Intelligence Council.

17 While the poverty rate in East Asia and the Pacific was estimated at 12.5% in 2010, it was over 30% for South Asia and close to 50% in Sub-Saharan Africa. IMF and World Bank. 2013. *Global Monitoring Report 2013. Rural-Urban Dynamics and the Millennium Development Goals.* Washington, DC, International Bank for Reconstruction and Development and the World Bank.

likely to have limited or no access to social security or secure income than wage and salaried workers.[18]

The lack of basic social protection in most countries is exacerbating such problems and contributing to rising inequality, both across and within the majority of countries in the global North, as well as in the global South.[19] The past quarter of a century has seen wealth become ever more concentrated in the hands of fewer people.[20] The wealth of the world is divided thus: almost half to the richest one per cent, the other half to the remaining 99 per cent.[21] Such rapidly widening income inequality is contributing to social exclusion and undermining social cohesion. In all societies, extreme inequalities are a source of social tension and a potential catalyst of political instability and violent conflict.

Box 1. High income inequality in Latin America despite strong economic growth

Latin America and the Caribbean remains one of the regions with the highest levels of income inequality, and this despite strong economic growth and improved social indicators observed over the past decade. The report observed that: 'Declines in the wage share have been attributed to the impact of labour-saving technological change and to a general weakening of labour market regulations and institutions. Such declines are likely to affect individuals in the middle and bottom of the income distribution disproportionately, since they rely mostly on labour income.' In addition, the report noted that 'highly-unequal land distribution has created social and political tensions and is a source of economic inefficiency, as small landholders frequently lack access to credit and other resources to increase productivity, while big owners may not have had enough incentive to do so.'

Source: UN Department of Economic and Social Affairs, 2013. *Inequality Matters. Report of the World Social Situation 2013*. New York, United Nations.

Growing interconnectedness, but rising intolerance and violence

The development of new digital technologies has resulted in an exponential growth in the volume of information and knowledge available, and made them more readily accessible to greater numbers of people throughout the world. As such, information and communication technologies can play an essential role in the sharing of knowledge and expertise in the service of sustainable development and in a spirit of solidarity. And yet, for many observers, the world is witnessing rising levels of ethnic, cultural and religious intolerance, often using the same communication technologies for ideological and political mobilization to promote exclusivist worldviews. This mobilization often leads to further criminal and political violence and to armed conflict.

---

18 International Labour Office. 2014. *Global Employment Trends 2014*. Geneva, International Labour Office.
19 UN DESA. 2013. *Inequality matters. Report on the World Social Situation 2013*. New York, United Nations.
20 See World Economic Forum. 2014. *Outlook on the Global Agenda 2015*. Global Agenda Councils. pp. 8-10.
21 Oxfam. 2014. Working for the Few: Political capture and economic inequality. *Oxfam Briefing Paper* No. 178. Oxford, UK, Oxfam.

Violence against women and girls tends to increase in times of crisis and instability, both during and after periods of upheaval and displacement caused by armed conflict. In such situations violence against women is widespread and may be systematic when rape, forced prostitution or sex trafficking are used by armed groups as a tactic of warfare.[22] Women are also more likely to be internally displaced, resulting in poor health and educational achievements,[23] which also has a direct effect on the treatment and condition of families and children.

Violence – including criminal violence linked to drug production and trafficking (extreme problems in certain parts of the world such as Central America), political instability and armed conflict – continues to threaten lives and to prevent social and economic development.[24] It is estimated that some 500 million people live in countries at risk of instability and conflict.[25] The economic impact of containing and dealing with the consequences of global violence has been estimated at close to 10 trillion US dollars: more than 11 per cent of global GDP, or twice the combined GDP of African countries in 2013.[26] Furthermore, the share of public budgets invested in security and the military diverts significant resources from development. Global military expenditures have continued to grow since 2000, reaching 1,742 billion US dollars worldwide in 2012[27], and a number of countries devote a greater share of their GDP to military spending than to education.

All this has important implications for the design and implementation of conflict-sensitive educational policies. These need to be inclusive, both in their formulation and in their implementation, if education is not simply to reproduce inequalities and social tensions that may be catalysts of violence and political instability. Human rights education has an important role to play in raising awareness about the issues that give rise to conflict and the means to its just resolution. Such education is important to promote the key principle of non-discrimination and the protection of life and human

---

22 UN Women. 2013. *A Transformative Stand-alone Goal on Achieving Gender Equality, Women's Rights and Women's Empowerment*. New York, UN Women.

23 World Bank. 2011. *World Development Report 2011: Conflict, Security and Development*. Washington, DC, The World Bank.

24 Markets for drugs are mainly found in the developed world, but it is countries in the developing world that are involved in their production, transformation, and traffic. The market is large and growing, and consequently so is the drug industry. Violence accompanies the drug industry because rival groups fight for territories. The drug industry is labour-intensive, needing untrained personnel to carry out many of its activities. In many countries, it is mainly young boys who join the trade. This implies dropping out of education and placing their lives in continuous danger, in exchange for attractive payments. Drug production entails the occupation of large territories and the domination of the resident population. Also, drug trafficking leads to other criminal activities – extortion, human trafficking and sexual slavery, kidnapping, etc. – that in general place personal security at risk in many places. Central American countries, Mexico, Columbia and some countries in western Asia are victims of this scourge. A solution to this problem is yet to be found.

25 Global Peace Index and Institute for Economics and Peace. 2014. *Global Peace Index 2014*. Institute for Economics and Peace.

26 Ibid.

27 Figures are in constant (2011) US$ prices and exchange rates. SIPRI Database, www.sipri.org/research/armaments/milex [Accessed February 2015].

dignity of all in times of violence and crisis. This requires the guarantee of safe, non-violent, inclusive and effective learning environments for all.

Human rights: Progress and challenges

Universal human rights are a collective aspiration towards a common ideal, whereby human beings are respected in their dignity independently of other differences and distinctions, and full opportunities are provided for their full development.[28] However, the gap observed between the adoption of international normative frameworks and their implementation represents a growing tension between the dynamics of power and the rule of rights codified as law. The aspiration to establish the rule of law and justice, both internationally and nationally, is frustrated in several instances by the hegemony of powerful interest groups. The challenge is how to ensure universal human rights through the rule of law, as well as through social, cultural and ethical norms.

Gender has long been a key element in discrimination. Women's rights have been strengthened over the past few decades, notably through efforts to expand the application of the 1979 Convention on the Elimination of All Forms of Discrimination against Women (CEDAW) and the implementation of the Framework for Action of the International Conference of Beijing (1995). Yet while considerable progress has been made in ensuring greater gender equality in access to health and to education, much less progress has been made in enhancing the voice and participation of women in social, economic and political life.[29] The majority of those living in extreme poverty are women.[30] They also constitute the majority of the world's illiterate youth and adults.[31] Moreover, women occupy less than 20 per cent of parliamentary seats worldwide.[32] The initially fragile situation of women in the labour market, and particularly in the informal sector, is becoming more precarious in the face of the brutal competition for jobs resulting from reduced employment opportunities, and the impact of successive economic and financial crises. Currently, half of the women in the labour force are in vulnerable employment, with no job security and no protection against economic shocks.[33] This adds to existing patterns of discrimination against women in salaries and career prospects.

---

28   The universality of human rights was first set out in the 1948 Universal Declaration and later by the Charter of Human Rights composed of successive conventions adopted by the United Nations and ratified by governments.
29   UN. 2013. *A New Global Partnership: Eradicate poverty and transform economies through sustainable development*, Report of the High-level Panel of eminent persons on the post-2015 development agenda. New York, United Nations.
30   Ibid.
31   UNESCO. 2014. *Teaching and Learning: Achieving quality for all. EFA Global Monitoring Report 2013-2014.* Paris, UNESCO.
32   UN Women. 2011. *Progress of the World's Women: In Pursuit of Justice.* New York, UN Women.
33   ILO. 2012. *Global Employment Trends for Women.* Geneva, ILO.

■ New knowledge horizons

The cyber world

One of the defining features of development today is the emergence and expansion of the cyber world, stimulated by the spectacular growth in internet connectivity and mobile penetration.[34] We live in a connected world. An estimated 40 per cent of the world's population now uses the internet and this number is growing at a remarkable rate.[35] While there are significant variations in internet connectivity among countries and regions, the number of households with such links in the global South has now overtaken those in the global North. Moreover, over 70 per cent of mobile telephone subscriptions worldwide are now in the global South.[36] Five billion people are expected to go from no to full connectivity within the next twenty years.[37] However, there are still significant gaps among countries and regions, for example between urban and rural areas. Limited broadband speed and lack of connectivity hamper access to knowledge, participation in society and economic development.

The internet has transformed how people access information and knowledge, how they interact, and the direction of public management and business. Digital connectivity holds promise for gains in health, education, communication, leisure and well-being.[38] Artificial intelligence advances, 3D printers, holographic recreation, instant transcription, voice-recognition and gesture-recognition software are only some examples of what is being tested. Digital technologies are reshaping human activity from daily life to international relations, from work to leisure, redefining multiple aspects of our private and public life.

Such technologies have expanded opportunities for freedom of expression and for social, civic and political mobilization, but they also raise important concerns. The availability of personal information in the cyber world, for example, brings up significant issues of privacy and security. New spaces for communication and socialization are transforming what constitutes the idea of 'social' and they require enforceable legal and other safeguards to prevent their overuse, abuse and misuse.[39] Examples of such misuse of the internet, mobile technology and social media range from cyber-bullying to criminal activity, even to terrorism. In this new cyber world, educators need to

---

34 International Telecommunication Union. 2013. *Trends in Telecommunication Reform: Transnational aspects of regulation in a networked society*. Geneva, International Telecommunication Union.
35 ITU. 2013. *The world in 2014: Fact and Figures*. Geneva, ITU.
36 ITU. 2014. *Trends in Telecommunication Reform, Special Edition. Fourth-generation regulation*. Geneva, ITU.
37 Schmidt, E. and Cohen, J. 2013. *The New Digital Age: Reshaping the Future of People, Nations and Business*. New York, Knopf.
38 Ibid.
39 Hart, A.D. and Hart Frejd, S. 2013. *The Digital Invasion: How Technology Is Shaping You and Your Relationships*. Ada, MI, Baker Books.

better prepare new generations of 'digital natives'[40] to deal with the ethical and social dimensions of not only existing digital technologies but also those yet to be invented.

Advances in the neurosciences

Recent developments in the neurosciences are increasingly attracting the interest of the education community seeking to better understand the interactions between biological processes and human learning. While it may still be premature for such developments to inform education policy, their potential to improve teaching and learning practices shows great promise. For example, the latest insights into how the brain develops and operates at different stages in life are contributing to our understanding of how and when we learn.

Some of the most significant insights concern the 'sensitive periods' of learning activities[41], indicating language acquisition is at its peak at an early age. This underlines the importance of early childhood education and the potential for multiple language learning in the early years. Other findings point to the 'plasticity' of the brain and its capacity to change in response to environmental demands throughout life.[42] This supports the idea of lifelong learning and the provision of appropriate learning opportunities for all regardless of age.

In addition, we must acknowledge the impact of environmental factors such as nutrition, sleep, sport and recreation on optimal brain functioning. Equally important, we must acknowledge the need for holistic approaches that recognize the close interdependence of physical and intellectual well-being, as well as the interplay of the emotional and cognitive, analytical and creative brain. The new research directions in neurosciences will add to our understanding of the nature-nurture relationship, helping us thereby to fine-tune our educational initiatives.

Climate change and alternative energy sources

Climate change is one of the defining challenges of this century, in terms of both the responses required to address it, and the means necessary to face its adverse impacts. Mitigation efforts call for a concerted engagement to contain emissions and prevent further drastic consequences on the planet; adaptation entails reducing vulnerabilities and building resilience to its impacts. Education plays a paramount role in raising awareness and promoting behavioural change for both climate change mitigation and adaptation.[43]

---

40 Prensky, M. 2001. Digital Natives, Digital Immigrants. *On the horizon*. MCB University Press, Vol. 9, No. 5.
41 OECD 2007. *Understanding the brain: The birth of a learning science*. Paris, EDUCERI-OECD.
42 Ibid.
43 Lutz, W., Muttarak, R. and Striessnig, E. 2014. Universal education is key to enhanced climate adaptation. *Science*. 28 November 2014. Vol. 346, No. 6213. Education is key to climate adaptation. www.iiasa.ac.at/web/home/about/news/20141127-Science-Pop.html [Accessed February 2015].

Education is a key factor in promoting and facilitating the collective transition to using alternative non-carbon renewable sources, which can mitigate the adverse impact of climate change. To make the shift away from carbon to non-carbon energy sources, we need to change beliefs and perceptions and foster mind sets that facilitate the transition. Energy infrastructure by itself will not result in the appropriate changes.

At the same time, education represents a key component of adaptive capacity, as the knowledge, skills and behaviours necessary to adapt lives and livelihoods to the ecological, social and economic realities of a changing environment must be transmitted to the present and next generations. The 2014 Lima Ministerial Declaration on Education and Awareness-raising encourages 'governments to develop education strategies that incorporate the issue of climate change in curricula and to include awareness-raising on climate change in the design and implementation of national development and climate change strategies and policies in line with their national priorities and competencies.'

Creativity, cultural innovation and youth

New forms of cultural and artistic expression have emerged in recent years. These are the result of acculturation impelled by the growth of connectivity and cultural exchange worldwide. The process is driven largely by young people. We see a new public aesthetic being expressed, rich in its inherent plurality, and we encounter a new willingness to innovate with form in each of the domains the youth inhabit, from fashion to food, music and personal relationships. The more than one billion young people between the ages of 15 and 24 in the world today are the most informed, active, connected and mobile generation the world has ever seen.[44] It is estimated that over 90 per cent of young people between the ages of 18 and 24 in the world today are on some form of social media, such as Facebook and Twitter. They spend considerable time on social media exploring and sharing the results of this exploration. This generates an environment of greater awareness and understanding of other cultures and an engagement with issues of aesthetics worldwide, leading to a recognition of the importance of other knowledge systems. Cultural diversity has become increasingly relevant as a source of invention and innovation; it is today a valuable resource for sustainable human development.[45]

---

[44]   'Youth-support' by Chernor Bah, Chair, Youth Advocacy Group for Global Education First Initiative (GEFI); Panel discussions: 'Enabling conditions for the delivery of quality global citizenship education: Where are we? Where do we want to go?' Global Citizenship Education: Enabling Conditions & Perspectives, 16 May 2014, UNESCO, Paris. www.unesco.org/new/fileadmin/MULTIMEDIA/HQ/ED/pdf/Chernor-Bah_16May2014.pdf [Accessed February 2015].

[45]   UNESCO. 2009. *UNESCO World Report Investing in Cultural Diversity and Intercultural Dialogue*. Paris, UNESCO. http://unesdoc.unesco.org/images/0018/001852/185202e.pdf [Accessed February 2015].

■ Exploring alternative approaches

Acknowledging the diversity of worldviews in a plural world

Exploring alternative approaches to human progress and well-being is crucial as we confront the complexity of current development patterns. It is important to highlight the diversity of societies, both in the global North and in the global South. Cultural diversity is humanity's greatest source of creativity and wealth. It entails diverse ways of viewing the world. It provides different approaches to solving problems that affect us all and valuing fundamental aspects of life: the natural ecosystem, the community, the individual, religion and spirituality. We must recognize the diversity of lived realities while reaffirming a common core of universal values. Because diversity makes any international definition and approach difficult to achieve, perspectives that look beyond traditional indicators of health, education and income are very welcome. Unfortunately, the subjective and contextual dimensions inherent to such diverse conceptions of human well-being continue to make many current policy approaches partial and inadequate.[46]

> We must recognize the diversity of lived realities while reaffirming a common core of universal values.

---

[46] While there is no shared understanding of what the notion of 'well-being' entails at the international level, it is now well-established that recourse to traditional socio-economic indicators is far from sufficient. The United Nations Development Program (UNDP) has recently gone beyond the Human Development Index (HDI), which integrates indicators relative to income, health and educational status. Concern for growing inequality and gender issues have seen further elaborations in terms of the Inequality-adjusted Human Development Index (IHDI), the Gender Development Index (GDI), and the Gender Inequality Index (GII). Attempts to go beyond indicators inspired by a very narrow conception of human progress include a range of initiatives exploring alternative measures of inclusion and sustainability at the global level. The Inclusive Wealth Index proposed by the United Nations University is one example being proposed. Others are: Better Life Initiative (OECD); EDP: Environmentally Adjusted Net Domestic Product (UN SEEA93); EPI: Environmental Performance Index (Yale University); ESI: Environmental Sustainability Index (Yale University); GPI: Genuine Progress Indicators (Redefining Progress); Green Growth Indicators (OECD); Genuine Savings (Pearce, Atkinson & Hamilton); HCI: Human Capital Index (World Economic Forum); ISEW: Index of Sustainable Economic Welfare (Cobb & Daly); NNW: Net National Welfare (Japanese Government); SDI: Sustainable Development Indicators (EU; UK Government).

Box 2. The encounter of diverse knowledge systems

The European culture has come to us not only with its own knowledge but with its velocity. Though our assimilation of it is imperfect and the consequent aberrations numerous, still it is rousing our intellectual life from its inertia of formal habits into glowing consciousness by the very contradiction it offers to our own mental traditions. What I object to is the artificial arrangement by which this foreign education tends to occupy all the space of our national mind and thus kills, or hampers, the great opportunity for the creation of a new thought power by a new combination of truths. It is this which makes me urge that all the elements in our own culture have to be strengthened, not to resist the Western culture, but truly to accept and assimilate it, and use it for our food and not as our burden; to get mastery over this culture, and not live at its outskirts as the hewers of texts and the drawers of book-learning.

Source: Tagore, R. 1996. The Centre of Indian Culture. Sisir Kumar Das (ed.), *The English Writings of Rabindranath Tagore*, Vol. 2, *Plays, Stories, Essays*. New Delhi, Sahitya Akademi, p. 486.

Integrating alternative knowledge systems

Alternatives to the dominant model of knowledge must be explored. Alternative knowledge systems need to be recognized and properly accounted for, rather than relegated to an inferior status. Societies everywhere can learn a great deal from each other by being more open to the discovery and understanding of other worldviews.

> Alternative knowledge systems need to be recognized and properly accounted for, rather than relegated to an inferior status.

There is much to learn, for instance, from rural societies across the world, particularly indigenous ones, about the relationship of human society to the natural environment. In many indigenous cultures, the Earth is considered the Mother. It or any of its products cannot be damaged without a valid reason, most often relating to survival. In many cultures, the human being is considered a member of nature, equal in rights and not superior to other living beings. Many rural societies have circular conceptions of time, not linear ones; they are linked to agricultural production, the progression of the seasons, and festivities and rituals that enhance the spiritual well-being of communities. In the same way, approaches to collective decision-making differ. Some societies have recourse to democracy and to voting to make collective decisions, even when in small groups; other societies seek consensus, which means argument, discussion and convincing. An endless array of different worldviews is available for the enrichment of all, if we are willing to abandon our certainties and open our minds to the possibilities of different explanations of reality.

It is essential to recall – as have thinkers Frantz Fanon, Aimé Césaire, Rabindranath Tagore and others – that when we privilege one form of knowledge, we in fact privilege a system of power. The future of education and development in today's world requires fostering a dialogue among different worldviews with the aim of integrating knowledge systems originating in diverse realities, and to establish our common heritage. Voices from the global South need to be heard in international debates on education. For example, in Andean communities in Latin America development is expressed through the notion of *sumak kawsay*, the Quechua word for '*buen vivir*', or 'good living'. Rooted in indigenous cultures and worldviews, *sumak kawsay* has been proposed as an alternative conception of development, and has been incorporated into the constitutions of Ecuador and Bolivia. Mahatma Gandhi's concept of 'trusteeship', by which we hold the Earth's wealth not as 'owners' but as 'trustees' of all living creatures and future generations, is also worth considering.[47]

Box 3. *Sumak Kawsay*: An alternative view of development

The concept of *sumak kawsay* is rooted in the worldview of the Quechua peoples of the Andes in Ecuador. Referred to as '*buen vivir*' in Spanish, the concept of *sumak kawsay* translates loosely in English as 'good living' or 'well living'. It connotes a harmonious collective development that conceives the individual within the context of the social and cultural communities and his or her natural environment. Rooted in the indigenous belief system of the Quechua, the concept incorporates western critiques of dominant development models to offer an alternative paradigm based on harmony between human beings, as well as between human beings and their natural environments.

The concept has inspired the recent revision of the Constitution of Ecuador which refers to a 'new form of public co-existence, in diversity and in harmony with nature, to achieve the good way of living, the sumak kawsay'. The Constitution is based on the recognition of the 'right of the population to live in a healthy and ecologically balanced environment that guarantees sustainability and the good way of living (sumak kawsay)'. The Constitution further specifies that the following shall be a responsibility of the State: 'To promote the generation and production of knowledge, to foster scientific and technological research, and to upgrade ancestral wisdom to thus contribute to the achievement of the good way of living (sumak kawsay).'[48]

Re-visioning education in a diverse world

The purpose of education must therefore be revisited in light of a renewed vision of sustainable human and social development that is both equitable and viable. This

---

47   M. K. Gandhi, 1960. *Trusteeship*. Compiled by Ravindra Kelekar. Ahemadabad, India, Jitendra T. Desai Navajivan Mudranalaya.

48   See Articles no. 14 and no. 387 of the Constitution of Ecuador: Art. 14 - Se reconoce el derecho de la población a vivir en un ambiente sano y ecológicamente equilibrado, que garantice la sostenibilidad y el buen vivir, sumak kawsay; Art. 387.- Será responsabilidad del Estado: [...] 2. Promover la generación y producción de conocimiento, fomentar la investigación científica y tecnológica, y potenciar los saberes ancestrales, para así contribuir a la realización del buen vivir, al sumak kawsay.

vision of sustainability must take into consideration the social, environmental and economic dimensions of human development and the various ways in which these relate to education: 'An empowering education is one that builds the human resources we need to be productive, to continue to learn, to solve problems, to be creative, and to live together and with nature in peace and harmony. When nations ensure that such an education is accessible to all throughout their lives, a quiet revolution is set in motion: education becomes the engine of sustainable development and the key to a better world.'[49] Education can, and must, contribute to a new vision of sustainable global development.

Box 4. Promoting sustainable development through education

'Education, including formal education, public awareness and training, should be recognized as a process by which human beings and societies can reach the fullest potential. Education is critical for promoting sustainable development and improving the capacity of people to address environment and development issues.'

Agenda 21, Article 36, Paragraph 3. 1992.

The 2014 Aichi-Nagoya Declaration on Education for Sustainable Development invites governments 'to reinforce the integration of ESD into education, training, and sustainable development policies.'

All forms of organized learning can be both adaptive and transformative. Basic education of good quality and further learning and training are essential to enable individuals and communities to adapt to environmental, social and economic change at local and global levels. But learning is also crucial for empowerment and the development of capabilities to effect social transformation. Indeed, education can contribute to the more challenging task of transforming our mind-set and our worldview. Education is central to developing the capabilities required to expand the opportunities people need to lead meaningful lives in equal dignity. A renewed vision of education should include developing critical thinking, independent judgement and debate. Improvements in the quality of education, and in the provision of economically and socially relevant learning as determined by individuals and communities, are intrinsic to making these shifts.

> Dominant utilitarian conceptions of education should accede to the expression of other ways of understanding human well-being, and thus, to a focus on the relevance of education as a common good.

The right to *quality* education is *the right to meaningful and relevant learning*. However, learning needs vary across communities in a diverse world. Relevant learning must

---

49   Power, C. 2015. *The Power of Education: Education for All, Development, Globalisation and UNESCO.* London, Springer.

therefore reflect what each culture, each human group, defines as what is required to live in dignity. We must accept that there are many different ways of defining the quality of life, and thus very diverse ways of defining what needs to be learned. Dominant utilitarian conceptions of education should accede to the expression of other ways of understanding human well-being, and thus, to a *focus on the relevance* of education as a *common good*. This implies hearing the silent voices of those who have not yet been heard. The immense wealth that such diversity represents can enlighten us all in our collective quest for well-being. A humanistic perspective is a necessary basis of alternative approaches to education and human well-being.

2. Reaffirming a humanistic approach

2. Reaffirming a humanistic approach

"My humanity is bound up in yours,
for we can only be human together."

Desmond Tutu, South African social rights activist and bishop

Sustaining and enhancing the dignity, capacity and welfare of the human person, in relation to others and to nature, should be the fundamental purpose of education in the twenty-first century. Such an aspiration may be designated *humanism*, which it should be UNESCO's mission to develop both conceptually and in practice. The concept of humanism has a long tradition in UNESCO. As far back as 1953, UNESCO published the proceedings of an international round-table discussion on 'Humanism and Education in East and West' that it had convened in New Delhi.[50]

The concept of humanism also has a long tradition in diverse cultures and religious traditions, as well as numerous and differing philosophical interpretations. For instance, one prominent interpretation of humanism has identified it with atheism and secular rationalism. This was extended to other philosophies, such as phenomenology or existentialism, which see an ontological difference between humanity and the rest of the natural world. However, there are also powerful religious interpretations of humanism that view humankind's achievements – educational, cultural and scientific – as mature examples of its relationship to nature, the universe and a Creator. In the late twentieth and early twenty-first centuries, criticisms of both anthropocentric and theocentric humanisms have come from post-modernists, some feminists, ecologists

---

[50]   UNESCO Unity and Diversity of Cultures. 1953. *Humanism and Education in East and West: An international round-table discussion.* Paris, UNESCO.

and, more recently, from those who see themselves as trans-humanists or even post-humanists, with their calls for biological selection and radical enhancement.

Each of these interpretations raises fundamental moral and ethical issues that are clearly matters of educational concern.

■ A humanistic approach to education

A humanistic vision reaffirms a set of universal ethical principles that should be the foundation for an integrated approach to the purpose and organization of education for all. Such an approach has implications for the design of learning processes that promote the acquisition of relevant knowledge and the development of competencies in the service of our common humanity. A humanistic approach takes the debate on education beyond its utilitarian role in economic development. It has a central concern for inclusiveness and for an education that does not exclude and marginalize. It serves as a guide to dealing with the transformation of the global learning landscape, one in which the role of teachers and other educators continues as central to facilitating learning for the sustainable development of all.

Countering dominant development discourse

As we address the larger question of the aims and purposes of education and the type of society to which we aspire, we need to consider cultural, social, economic, ethical and civic dimensions. The economic functions of education are undoubtedly important, but we must go beyond the strictly utilitarian vision and the human capital approach that characterizes much of international development discourse.[51] Education is not only about the acquisition of skills, it is also about values of respect for life and human dignity required for social harmony in a diverse world. Understanding that ethical issues are fundamental to the development process can counter the current dominant discourse. Such an understanding enhances the role of education in developing the capabilities required for people to lead meaningful and dignified lives in line with Amartya Sen's alternative view of development.[52]

An integrated approach based on sound ethical and moral foundations

It is necessary, therefore, to reassert a humanistic approach to learning throughout life for social, economic and cultural development. Naturally, focus on particular dimensions may shift in different learning settings and at different stages of the life course. But in reaffirming the relevance of lifelong learning as the organizing principle for education,

---

[51] The two pages devoted to education in the 2013 High-Level Panel report on post-2015 development, for instance, are couched in the language of the human capital approach, referring to returns on investment in education and its contribution to the formation of 'productive citizens'.

[52] Sen, A. 1999. *Development as Freedom*. New York, Random House; Sen, A. 1999. *Commodities and Capabilities*. New Delhi, Oxford University Press.

it is critical to integrate the social, economic and cultural dimensions.[53] A humanistic approach to education goes beyond the notion of *scientific humanism*, which was proposed as the guiding principle for UNESCO by its first Director-General Julian Huxley and taken up in the 1972 Faure Report.[54] As noted above, the concept of *humanism* has given rise to several, often conflicting, interpretations, each of which raises fundamental moral and ethical issues that are clearly matters of educational concern. It can be argued that sustaining and enhancing the dignity, capacity and welfare of the human person in relation to others, and to nature, should be the fundamental purpose of education in the twenty-first century.[55] The humanistic values that should be the foundations and purpose of education include: *respect for life and human dignity, equal rights and social justice, cultural and social diversity,* and a *sense of human solidarity and shared responsibility for our common future.* A dialogical approach to learning is required, as encouraged, for instance, by Martin Buber[56] and Paulo Freire.[57] We also have to reject learning systems that alienate individuals and treat them as commodities, and of social practices that divide and dehumanize people. It is crucial to educate in such values and principles if we are to achieve sustainability and peace.

> Sustaining and enhancing the dignity, capacity and welfare of the human person in relation to others, and to nature, should be the fundamental purpose of education in the twenty-first century.

By broadening its scope in these ways, education can be transformative and contribute to a sustainable future for all. Based on this ethical foundation, critical thinking, independent judgement, problem-solving, and information and media literacy skills are the keys to developing transformative attitudes. An integrated and humanistic approach to education, as that presented in the 1996 Delors Report, is all the more relevant in today's world where sustainability has become a central concern of global development. The dimensions of sustainable development, in which economic growth is guided by environmental stewardship and concern for social justice, require an integrated approach to education that addresses multiple social, ethical, economic, cultural, civic and spiritual dimensions.

---

53 It is worth noting that the proposed education-related sustainable development goal beyond 2015 is framed in terms of lifelong learning: 'Ensure inclusive and equitable quality education and promote lifelong learning opportunities for all'. https://sustainabledevelopment.un.org/content/documents/1579SDGs%20Proposal.pdf [Accessed February 2015].

54 See Huxley, J. 1946. *UNESCO: Its purpose and philosophy.* Paris, UNESCO Preparatory Commission; and, the recent reference to this in Haddad, G. and Aubin, J. P. 2013. Toward a humanism of knowledge, action and cooperation. *International Review of Education*, Vol. 59, No. 3, pp. 331-341.

55 See for example the collection of articles in 'On Dignity', *Diogenes*, August 2007, Nol. 54, No. 3, http://dio.sagepub.com/content/54/3.toc#content-block [Accessed February 2015].

56 Morgan, W. J. and Guilherme, A. 2014. *Buber and Education: Dialogue as conflict resolution.* London, Routledge.

57 See, for example, Roberts, P. 2000. *Education, Literacy, and Humanization: Exploring the work of Paulo Freire.* Westport, CT and London, Bergin and Garvey.

We need a holistic approach to education and learning that overcomes the traditional dichotomies between cognitive, emotional and ethical aspects. Overcoming the dichotomy between cognitive and other forms of learning is increasingly being recognized as essential to education. This is true even among those who focus on the measurement of learning achievement in school education. More holistic assessment frameworks have recently been proposed that go beyond traditional domains of academic learning to include, for example, social and emotional learning or culture and the arts.[58] These attempts indicate the recognized need to go beyond conventional academic learning, despite the serious reservations about the feasibility of capturing such important emotional, social and ethical learning though measurement, especially at the global level.

Reinterpreting and protecting the four pillars of education

One of the most influential concepts of the 1996 Delors Report was that of the *four pillars of learning*. Formal education, the report argued, tends to emphasize certain types of knowledge to the detriment of others that are essential to sustaining human development. It affirmed that equal attention should be paid, in all organized learning, to each of the four pillars:[59]

- Learning to know – a broad general knowledge with the opportunity to work in depth on a small number of subjects.
- Learning to do – to acquire not only occupational skills but also the competence to deal with many situations and to work in teams.
- Learning to be – to develop one's personality and to be able to act with growing autonomy, judgment and personal responsibility.
- Learning to live together – by developing an understanding of other people and an appreciation of interdependence.

The idea of the integrated approach to education reflected in the four pillars of learning has had significant influence on policy debates, teacher training and curriculum development in a range of countries worldwide. A recent example: the four pillars were used as the inspirational starting point of the Spanish Basque basic schooling curriculum and adapted for its development. These four pillars of learning remain relevant to an integrated approach to education. Their generic nature allows for interpretation of the type of integrated learning required in response to different contexts and times. The pillars themselves might need fresh interpretation, given growing concern for sustainability. *Learning to live together*, for example, must go beyond the social and cultural dimensions of human interaction to include a concern for the relationship of human society with the natural environment.

---

58 See, for instance, the work of the international Learning Metrics Task Force.
59 Delors, J. et al. 1996. *Learning: The treasure within*. Paris, UNESCO.

Of greater concern is that the four pillars of learning are fundamentally under threat in the context of current societal challenges, and particularly the pillars of *learning to be* and *to live together*, which best reflect the socialization function of education. The strengthening of ethical principles and values in the process of learning is essential to protecting these pillars of a humanistic vision of education.

> The four pillars of learning are fundamentally under threat in the context of current societal challenges, and particularly the pillars of *learning to be* and to *live together.*

Learning to learn and the development of competencies

Much international debate is taking place now about the types of skills and competencies required in the current context of complexity and uncertainty. However, the diverse and often overlapping definitions of skills and competencies, and the multiple ways of categorizing them, can create confusion. Although the terms *skills* and *competencies* are often used interchangeably, a clear difference exists between the two. Competencies are broader in scope. They refer to the ability to use knowledge – understood broadly as encompassing information, understanding, skills, values, and attitudes – in specific contexts and to meet demands.

Box 5. Foundation, transferable, and technical and vocational skills

The *EFA Global Monitoring Report 2012* proposes a useful approach to different types of skills in relation to the world of work. It identifies three main types of skills that all young people need – foundation, transferable, and technical and vocational skills – and the contexts in which they may be acquired:

Foundation skills: At their most elemental, foundation skills are the literacy and numeracy skills necessary for getting work that pays enough to meet daily needs. These foundations are also a prerequisite for engaging in further education and training, and for acquiring transferable skills and technical and vocational skills.

Transferable skills: Finding and keeping work require a broad range of skills that can be transferred and adapted to different work needs and environments. Transferable skills include analysing problems and reaching appropriate solutions, communicating ideas and information effectively, being creative, showing leadership and conscientiousness, and demonstrating entrepreneurial capabilities. Such skills are nurtured to some extent outside the school environment. They can, however, be further developed through education and training

Technical and vocational skills: Many jobs require specific technical know-how, whether related to growing vegetables, using a sewing machine, engaging in bricklaying or carpentry, or working on a computer in an office. Technical and vocational skills can be acquired through work placement programmes linked to secondary schooling and formal technical and vocational education, or through work-based training, including traditional apprenticeships and agricultural cooperatives.

Source: UNESCO. 2012. *Youth and Skills: Putting education to work. EFA Global Monitoring Report 2012.* Paris, UNESCO.

The focus on the importance of 'soft', 'transferable', 'non-cognitive' or 'twenty-first century' skills has enriched current thinking on educational content and methods. The underlying and often implicit rationale is the need for creativity and entrepreneurship for greater competitiveness. Although this rationale is key to the economic function of education, it must not overshadow the need to develop those competencies that individuals and communities require for the multiple dimensions of human existence – competencies that contribute to the empowerment of both. Competencies enhance the ability to use the appropriate knowledge (information, understanding, skills and values) creatively and responsibly in given situations to find solutions and establish new ties with others.

The knowledge required is not prescribed by a central authority, but identified through schools, teachers and communities. It is knowledge that is not merely transmitted but explored, researched, experimented with, and created according to human need. It is knowledge used for developing basic language and communication skills; for solving problems; and to develop higher-order skills such as logical thinking, analyzing, synthesizing, inferring, deducting, inducting, and thinking hypothetically. It is knowledge that is arrived at in ways that nurture what is perhaps the most important skill of all: the ability to access and critically process information. Learning to learn has never been as important as it is today.

> Learning to learn has never been as important as it is today.

The volume of information now available on the internet is staggering. The challenge becomes how to teach learners to make sense of the vast amount of information they encounter every day, identify credible sources, assess the reliability and validity of what they read, question the authenticity and accuracy of information, connect this new knowledge with prior learning and discern its significance in relation to information they already understand.[60]

Rethinking curriculum development

What would a humanistic curriculum look like from the perspective of policy formulation and content? Regarding learning content and methods, a humanistic curriculum is certainly one that raises more questions than it provides answers. It promotes respect for diversity and rejection of all forms of (cultural) hegemony, stereotypes and biases. It is a curriculum based on intercultural education that allows for the plurality of society while ensuring balance between pluralism and universal values. In terms of policy, we must recall that curriculum frameworks are tools to bridge broad educational goals and the processes to reach them. For curriculum frameworks to be legitimate, the process

---

[60] Facer, K. 2011. *Learning Futures: Education, Technology and Social Challenges*. New York, Routledge.

of policy dialogue to define educational goals must be participatory and inclusive.[61] Curriculum policy and content must both be guided by the principles of social and economic justice, equality and environmental responsibility that constitute the pillars of sustainable development.

■ Ensuring more inclusive education

Progress, but persistent inequalities in basic education

We have made significant progress in ensuring the right to basic education since 2000, in part driven by the Education for All (EFA) and the Millennium Development Goals (MDG) frameworks. This progress is reflected in improved school enrolment ratios, fewer out-of-school children, higher literacy rates particularly among youth, and a narrower gender gap in both school enrolment and adult literacy across the world.

Despite this progress, the pledge made as long ago as 1990 by governments and international development partners to 'meet the basic learning needs of all children, youth and adults' has not been kept. Close to 60 million children and 70 million adolescents worldwide still do not have access to effective basic education. In 2011, close to 775 million adults were still considered to have insufficient levels of literacy. Even for those with access to formal basic education, incomplete schooling and education of poor quality are contributing to insufficient levels of basic skills acquisition, with the quality of education and the relevance of learning remaining key concerns. At least 250 million children are still not able to read, write or count adequately even after at least four years in school.[62]

Furthermore, significant inequalities among countries persist and national averages in many countries mask striking inequalities within countries in levels of attainment and outcomes in basic education.[63] Traditional factors of marginalization in education such as gender and urban or rural residence continue to combine with income, language, minority status and disability to create 'mutually reinforcing disadvantages', particularly in low-income or conflict-affected countries.[64]

---

[61] Amadio, M., Opertti, R., Tedesco, J.C. 2014. Curriculum in the Twenty-First Century: Challenges, Tensions and Open Questions. *ERF Working Papers,* No. 9. Paris, UNESCO.
See also: International Bureau of Education UNESCO. 2013. The Curriculum Debate: Why It Is Important Today. *IBE Working Papers on Curriculum Issues* No. 10. Geneva, IBE UNESCO.
[62] UNESCO. 2014. *Teaching and Learning: Achieving quality for all. EFA Global Monitoring Report 2013-2014.* Paris, UNESCO.
[63] Extracted from Muscat Agreement (2014) which refers to GMR data. *More than 57 million children and 69 million adolescents still do not have access to effective basic education. In 2011, an estimated 774 million adults were illiterate.*
[64] UNESCO. 2011. *The hidden crisis: Armed conflict and education. EFA Global Monitoring Report 2011.* Paris, UNESCO.

Box 6. Children with disabilities are often overlooked

Children with disabilities are often denied their right to education. However, little is known about their school attendance patterns. The collection of data on children with disabilities is not straightforward, but data are vital to ensure that policies are in place to address the constraints these children face.

By one estimate, 93 million children under age 14, or 5.1% of the world's children, were living with a 'moderate or severe disability' in 2004. According to the World Health Survey, in 14 of 15 low and middle income countries, people of working age with disabilities were about one-third less likely to have completed primary school. For example, in Bangladesh, 30% of people with disabilities had completed primary school, compared with 48% of those with no disabilities. The corresponding shares were 43% and 57% in Zambia; 56% and 72% in Paraguay.

It has been shown that children with a higher risk of disability are far more likely to be denied a chance to go to school. In Bangladesh, Bhutan and Iraq, children with mental impairments were most likely to be denied this right. In Iraq, for instance, 10% of 6- to 9-year-olds with no risk of disability had never been to school in 2006, but 19% of those at risk of having a hearing impairment and 51% of those who were at higher risk of mental disability had never been to school. In Thailand, almost all 6- to 9-year-olds who had no disability had been to school in 2005/06, and yet 34% of those with walking or moving impairments had never been to school.

Source: UNESCO. 2014. *Teaching and Learning: Achieving quality for all. EFA Global Monitoring Report 2013-2014*: Paris, UNESCO.

Gender equality in basic education

Gender equality in education has traditionally been narrowly equated with gender parity at different levels of formal education. Gender has been a traditional factor of inequality and disparity in education, most often to the disadvantage of girls and women. Yet we note significant progress in narrowing the gap around the world since 2000, with a larger proportion of girls and women accessing different levels of formal education. Indeed, gender parity in primary education has been achieved in Central and Eastern Europe, Central Asia, East Asia and the Pacific, Latin America and the Caribbean, North America and Western Europe. In addition, significant progress has been made since 2000 in narrowing the gender gap, particularly in South and West Asia and to a lesser degree in sub-Saharan Africa and the Arab States. However, despite the significant progress made, the majority of out-of-school children are girls, while two-thirds of youth and adults with low levels of literacy in the world are women. To help ensure women's empowerment, boys and men must also be engaged in the fight against gender inequality. This must begin with basic education.

Box 7. Hearing the voice of girls deprived of education

Education is one of the blessings of life – and one of its necessities.
Today...I am not a lone voice, I am many.
I am those 66 million girls who are deprived of education.
And today I am not raising my voice. It is the voice of those 66 million girls.

Nobel Peace Prize acceptance speech by Malala Yousafzai, Oslo, 10 December 2014

Gender parity in secondary and higher education

In secondary education, the goal of gender parity has been achieved in a number of regions including Central Asia, East Asia, Latin America and the Caribbean, as well as North America and Western Europe. In other regions, the gender gap has been narrowing, particularly in South and West Asia and to a lesser degree in the Arab States. The gender gap in secondary enrolment is most evident in sub-Saharan Africa, Western Asia and South Asia where average enrolment ratios are the lowest. Regarding tertiary education, however, the proportion of women among university students in sub-Saharan Africa remains small and the goal of gender parity in tertiary education represents an important challenge. Elsewhere in the world, progress has been observed in most regions, with particularly striking progress in the Arab States, East Asia and the Pacific, and South and West Asia. In certain regions, such as Central and Eastern Europe, the Caribbean, North America, the Pacific, and Western Europe, the proportion of women participating in higher education is in fact greater than that of men. This is not only due to the faster growth of girls' enrolment in secondary education, but also to boys' underachievement in and lower completion of secondary education, observed in many regions. The pattern of boys' high drop-out from secondary education in some parts of the world such as the Caribbean and Latin America is another issue of concern because it puts further strain on social cohesion.

Education as a potential equalizer

Education often reproduces or even exacerbates inequalities, but it can also serve to equalize. Inclusive educational processes are essential for equitable development, and this appears to be true for various levels of educational provision.

Early childhood education: It is true, for instance, at the level of early childhood education where we note growing recognition of the foundational importance of early interventions for future learning and life chances. Research results demonstrate that early interventions for young children are essential not only for their own well-being: They also have sustainable, long-term effects on the development of human capital, social cohesion and economic success. Evidence shows that the most disadvantaged children – their disadvantage due, *inter alia,* to poverty, ethnic and linguistic minority status, gender discrimination, remoteness, disability, violence, and HIV/AIDS status –

experience the most dramatic gains from good quality Early Childhood Development programmes; yet it is exactly such children who are least likely to participate in these programmes.[65] Meta-reviews of early interventions identify one reason for their effectiveness: As children get older, the disparity between an average growth trajectory and a delayed trajectory widens. It is now well understood that intervening earlier requires fewer resources and less effort; at the same time, it is more effective. This is especially significant when providing for children with specific disabilities and special needs, for instance those with autism or Asperger syndrome.[66]

Box 8. Senegal: The 'Case des Tout-Petits' experience

The health and social status of children in Senegal is unfavourable and despite serious efforts the protection of children remains of great concern. In reaction to this situation, Senegalese national authorities now consider early childhood care a priority for development. Since 2002, the 'Case des Tout-Petits', a new model for the development of children in their early years, has coexisted alongside the various structures of formal, non-formal and informal pre-school education. While there is room for improvement, the programme is a valuable community-based experience grounded in local cultural traditions.

The 'Case des Tout-Petits' is a community structure for the support of children aged from 0 to 6. The *case*, or traditional house, connotes a lifestyle, a way of being and thinking, and symbolizes a commitment to African values. The *case* as a living, socialized, educational place *par excellence* is considered the starting point for the child's learning in life.

These 'cases' were primarily designed for disadvantaged and rural milieus to guarantee access to adequate and integrated services. They are run by the people themselves and represent some 20% of Senegal's early childhood structures. Architecturally, the 'Case des Tout-Petits' is a hexagonal structure comprising two rooms, one for the children's educational activities and the other for parental education. These structures develop a comprehensive and holistic approach to childhood care that includes education, health and nutrition programmes.

While participation is not free, fees are lower than in other early childhood care structures within the formal sector. The financial participation is symbolic and allows families to work in synergy around a common good that belongs to the community and that the community is expected to preserve.

Source: Adapted from Turpin Bassama, S., 2010. La case des tout-petits au Sénégal. *Revue Internationale d'éducation de Sèvres*. No. 53-2010, pp. 65–75.

Secondary education: It may also be true for secondary and tertiary education. Expansion of access to basic schooling worldwide has increased demand for secondary and tertiary education and concern for vocational skills development, particularly in a context of growing youth unemployment and a process of qualification

---

65   Global Child Development Group. 2011. *Child Development Lancet Series: Executive Summary.* www.globalchilddevelopment.org [Accessed February 2015].
66   Baron-Cohen, S. 2008. *The Facts: Autism and Asperger Syndrome.* Oxford, UK, Oxford University Press.

and requalification. In some countries in the Latin America and the Caribbean regions, for instance, the expansion of post-basic educational opportunities combined with pro-poor public policies have been shown to reduce inequality: 'Investment in education, labour market institutions and regulations can change patterns of inequality. In those Latin American countries where inequality has declined, two key factors have contributed to such declines: the expansion of education, and public transfers to the poor.... Increase in public expenditure on education throughout Latin America and the Caribbean, for instance, is leading to rising secondary enrolment and completion rates, and this is becoming a major determinant of the fall in inequality.'[67]

Higher education: Access to higher education has known a spectacular expansion over the past fifteen years. Global enrolment in tertiary education has doubled since 2000 with today some 200 million students worldwide, half of whom are women.[68] However, disparities based on income and other factors of social marginalization remain widespread, and this despite a variety of policy measures in recent years. Learners from higher income groups have retained their relative advantage in access to tertiary education across the world. Even in countries with high enrolment rates, the participation of minorities continues to lag behind the national average. It is important to note in this respect that most of the growth in higher education has been and continues to be in the private sector. The growing share of private institutions and the trend towards the privatization of the public sector worldwide have implications for access and equity. Direct and indirect costs of studies in higher education remain the main cause of exclusion. While loan programmes are attractive, they are not widespread.[69]

---

67   UN DESA. 2013. *Inequality Matters*. Report of the World Social Situation 2013. New York, United Nations.
68   Based on UNESCO Institute of Statistics data.
69   Altbach, P. G., Reisberg, L. and Rumbley, L. E. 2009. *Trends in Global Higher Education: Tracking an Academic Revolution*. Paris, UNESCO. (Report Prepared for the UNESCO 2009 World Conference on Higher Education)

Box 9. Intercultural Universities in Mexico

While an estimated 10% of the population of Mexico is indigenous, it is the least represented in higher education. According to estimates, only between 1% and 3% of higher education enrollment in Mexico is indigenous.

In 2004, in response to this inequality, the General Coordination for Intercultural and Bilingual Education at the Ministry of Education established Intercultural Universities with the active participation of indigenous organizations and academic institutions in each region. These institutions are located in densely indigenous areas and, though they allow for diversity in enrolment, they are especially intended for the indigenous population. Founded on the principle of intercultural education, they aim to foster dialogue between different cultures and represent a way of responding to both the historical and more recent demands of indigenous peoples.

In congruence with the recognition of diversity, Intercultural Universities do not propose a fixed approach to their educational activities. While assuring the respect of some basic principles, each university defines its curriculum according to the needs and potentials of the region in which it is located. Students are engaged in activities that relate them to the surrounding communities through research and development projects, with the aim of working and contributing to the development of their territory, their people and their culture.

Twelve Intercultural Universities are currently operating with a total enrollment of approximately 7,000 students and a high proportion of female students. Despite the challenges of financing, of students' living conditions and of political vulnerability that these universities face, they represent an important contribution to the achievement of educational equity.

Source: Adapted from Schmelkes, S. 2009. Intercultural Universities in Mexico: Progress and difficulties. *Intercultural Education*, Vol. 20, No. 1, pp. 5-17. www.tandfonline.com/doi/full/10.1080/14675980802700649 [Accessed February 2015].

■ The transformation of the educational landscape

The educational landscape of today's world is undergoing radical transformation with regard to methods, content and spaces of learning. This is true both for schooling and higher education. The increased availability of and access to diverse sources of knowledge are expanding opportunities for learning, which may be less structured and more innovative, affecting the classroom, pedagogy, teacher authority and learning processes.

In scale, the current transformation of the learning landscape has been likened to the historical transition from the traditional pre-industrial educational model to the factory-model initiated in the nineteenth century. In the traditional pre-industrial model, most of what people learned came through the activities of their daily lives and work. In contrast, the model of mass education born of the industrial revolution equated learning – almost exclusively – with schooling. The schooling model, moreover, continues to associate learning essentially with classroom teaching, when in fact a lot of learning (even in traditional educational settings) takes place at home and elsewhere.

Nonetheless, the physical space defined by the classroom as the main locus of learning remains a central feature of formal education systems at all levels of learning.[70]

Is schooling really over?

Some now argue that the schooling model has no future in the digital age as a consequence of the opportunities offered by e-learning, mobile learning and other digital technologies. In this respect it would be worth revisiting the deschooling debates of the 1960s and of the 1970s, notably the work of Paul Goodman[71] and of Ivan Illich.[72] It is true the current industrial model of schooling was designed to meet the production needs of well over a century ago, that modes of learning have changed dramatically over the past two decades, and sources of knowledge have changed, as have the ways in which we exchange and interact with it. It is also true that formal education systems have been slow to change and remain remarkably similar to what they have been for the past two centuries.[73] And yet, schooling remains as important as ever. It is the first step in institutionalized learning and socialization beyond the family, and it is an essential component of social learning: *learning to be* and *learning to live together*. Learning should not be merely an individual process. As a social experience, it requires learning with and through others – through discussion and debate with both peers and teachers.

> What we need is a more fluid approach to learning as a continuum, in which schooling and formal education institutions interact more closely with other less formalized educational experiences from early childhood throughout life.

Towards networks of learning spaces

Nevertheless, the transformation of the educational landscape in the contemporary world has seen growing recognition of the importance and relevance of learning outside formal institutions. There is a move from traditional educational institutions towards mixed, diverse and complex learning landscapes in which formal, non-formal and informal learning occur through a variety of educational institutions and third-party providers.[74] What we need is a more fluid approach to learning as a continuum, in which schooling and formal education institutions interact more closely with other less formalized educational experiences from early childhood throughout life. The changes in the spaces, times and relations in which learning takes place favour a network of learning spaces where non-formal and informal spaces of learning will interact with and complement formal educational institutions.

---

70 Frey, T. 2010. The future of education. *FuturistSpeaker*. www.futuristspeaker.com/2007/03/the-future-of-education [Accessed February 2015].

71 Goodman, P. 1971. *Compulsory Miseducation*. Harmandsworth, UK, Penguin Books.

72 Illich, I. 1973. *Deschooling Society*. Harmandsworth, UK, Penguin Books.

73 Davidson, C.N. and Goldberg, D.T. with Jones, Z.M. 2009. *The Future of Learning Institutions in the Digital Age*. Cambridge, MA, MIT Press (MacArthur Foundation Report on Digital media and Learning).

74 Scott, C. 2015. The Futures of Learning. *ERF Working Papers*. Paris, UNESCO.

Emerging learning spaces

Classroom-centred learning is now challenged by the expansion of access to knowledge and the emergence of learning spaces beyond classrooms, schools, universities and other educational institutions.[75] Social media, for instance, can extend classroom work by providing opportunities for such activities as collaboration and co-authoring. Mobile devices enable learners to access educational resources, connect with others or create content, both inside and outside the classroom.[76] Similarly, Massive Open On-Line Courses (MOOCs) in higher education, where a consortium of universities comes together to pool faculty resources in providing course content, have opened up new avenues for reaching wider audiences in higher education across the world. The current context of transformation of the educational landscape offers an opportunity to reconcile all learning spaces by creating synergies between formal education and training institutions and other educational experiences. It also offers new opportunities for experimentation and innovation.

Box 10. The 'Hole-in-the-Wall' experiment

Dr Sugata Mitra, Chief Scientist at NIIT, is credited with the Hole-in-the-Wall experiment. As early as 1982, he had been toying with the idea of unsupervised learning and computers. Finally, in 1999, Dr Mitra's team carved a 'hole in the wall' that separated the NIIT premises from the adjoining slum in Kalkaji, New Delhi. Through this hole, a freely accessible computer was put up for use.

This computer proved to be an instant hit among the slum dwellers, especially the children. With no prior experience, the children learnt to use the computer on their own. This prompted the following hypothesis: The acquisition of basic computing skills by any set of children can be achieved through incidental learning provided the learners are given access to a suitable computing facility, with entertaining and motivating content and some minimal (human) guidance.

Encouraged by the success of the Kalkaji experiment, freely accessible computers were set up in Shivpuri (a town in Madhya Pradesh) and in Madantusi (a village in Uttar Pradesh). These experiments came to be known as Hole-in-the-Wall experiments. The findings from Shivpuri and Madantusi confirmed the results of Kalkaji experiments. It appeared that the children in these two places picked up computer skills on their own. This new way of learning has come to be known as Minimally Invasive Education.

Since its inception in 1999, the Hole-in-the-Wall experiment has grown from a single computer at Kalkaji, New Delhi, to more than a hundred computers at various locations - even some which are hugely remote and inaccessible – across India and abroad, including Bhutan, Cambodia and the Central African Republic.

Note: NIIT Limited is an Indian company based in Gurgaon, India, that operates several for-profit higher education institutions.

Source: Adapted from: www.hole-in-the-wall.com [Accessed February 2015]

---

[75] Hannon, V., Patton, A. and Temperley, J. 2011. *Developing an Innovation - Ecosystem for Education.* Indianapolis, CISCO; Taddei, F. 2009. *Training creative and collaborative knowledge-builders: A major challenge for 21st century education.* Report prepared for the OECD on the future of education. Paris, OECD.

[76] Grimus, M. and Ebner, M. 2013. M-Learning in Sub Saharan Africa Context- What is it about. *Proceedings of World Conference on Educational Multimedia, Hypermedia and Telecommunications 2013,* pp. 2028-2033. Chesapeake, VA: AACE.

Mobile learning

Recent interest in the use of mobile technologies for learning is considerable. Mobile learning, alone or in combination with other information and communication technologies, is said to enable learning anytime and anywhere.[77] These technologies are continuously evolving, and currently include mobile and smart phones, tablet computers, e-readers, portable audio players and hand-held consoles. The emergence of new technologies has drastically changed the nature of educational processes. Lightweight and portable devices – ranging from mobile phones, tablet PCs, to palmtops – have liberated learning from fixed and predetermined locations, changing the nature of knowledge in modern societies.[78] Learning has thus become more informal, personal and ubiquitous.[79] Mobile technologies are especially interesting for educators because of their lower cost in comparison with desktop computers, and their incorporation of rich resources from the internet.[80]

Gaining prominence in various education sectors, mobile learning has furthered basic and higher education, as well as connected formal and informal education.[81] Given their portability and low-cost features, inexpensive mobile learning devices have the potential to increase the accessibility and effectiveness of basic education.[82] Mobile technologies 'hold the key to turning today's digital divide into digital dividends bringing equitable and quality education for all.'[83] Notably, the development of mobile technologies has opened up many possibilities in literacy and language learning.[84] Research has demonstrated mobile technology's effectiveness in improving literacy performance among learners. Because mobile technology can reach a wider audience, it holds the promise of transforming education for children and youth in isolated and other underserved conditions.[85]

[77] UNESCO. 2013. *Policy Guidelines for mobile learning*. Paris, UNESCO.

[78] O'Malley, C., Vavoula, G., Glew, J.P., Taylor, J., Sharples, M. and Lefrere, P. 2003. *MOBIlearn WP4 - Guidelines for Learning/Teaching/Tutoring in a Mobile Environment*. www2.le.ac.uk/Members/gv18/gv-publications [Accessed February 2015].

[79] Traxler, J. 2009. Current State of Mobile Learning. M. Alley (ed.), *Mobile Learning: Transforming the Delivery of Education and Training* Athabasca, AB, Canada, AU Press. pp. 9-24.

[80] Kukulska-Hulme, A. 2005. Introduction. J. Traxler and A. Kukulska-Hulme (eds), *Mobile learning – A handbook for educators and trainers*, New York, Routledge, pp. 1-6.

[81] Traxler, op. cit.

[82] Kim, P.H. 2009. Action Research Approach on Mobile Learning Design for the Underserved. *Education Technology Research Development*. Vol. 57, No. 3, pp. 415-435.

[83] ITU and UNESCO. 2014. Mobile learning week: A revolution for inclusive and better education. UNESCO website. www.unesco.org/new/en/media-services/in-focus-articles/mobile-learning-week-a-revolution-for-inclusive-better-education [Accessed February 2015].

[84] Joseph, S., Uther, M. 2006. Mobile language learning with multimedia and multi-modal interfaces. *Proceedings of the fourth IEEE International Workshop on Wireless, Mobile and Ubiquitous Technology in Education* (ICHIT '06), pp. 124-128.

[85] Saechao, N. 2012. Harnessing Mobile Learning to Advance Global Literacy. *The Asia Foundation*. http://asiafoundation.org/in-asia/2012/09/05/harnessing-mobile-learning-to-advance-global-literacy/ [Accessed February 2015].

Box 11. Mobile literacy for girls in Pakistan

The UNESCO Mobile Literacy Project used mobile phones to complement and support a traditional face-to-face literacy course offered to 250 adolescent girls living in remote areas of Pakistan. Illiteracy is an acute problem in Pakistan and disproportionately impacts women and girls. Across the country the adult literacy rate is 69% for males but only 40% for females. Because education research shows that newly acquired literacy skills quickly atrophy without consistent practice, project planners wanted a way to support the girls remotely after they completed the course.

The only way to communicate with participating students who lived in villages without computers or reliable fixed-line internet connections was via mobile phones. Programme instructors sent text messages to their students reminding them to practice handwriting skills or reread passages in a workbook. Instructors also posed questions to their students, which the girls answered via text messages. All the activities and communication sought to reinforce the literacy skills the girls had gained during the in-person course.

Before the project incorporated mobile devices, only 28% of the girls who completed the literacy course earned an 'A' grade on a follow-up examination. However, with the mobile support over 60% of the girls earned an 'A' grade. Based on this initial success the project is currently being expanded and now reaches over 2,500 students.

Source: UNESCO. 2013. *Policy Guidelines for Mobile Learning*. Paris, UNESCO, p. 15.

Massive Open On-line Courses (MOOCs) – Promises and limits

Massive Open On-line Courses are also transforming the landscape of higher education to a certain degree. They have generated significant interest from governments, educational institutions and business groups.[86] Yet while MOOCs have become an important platform for expanding higher education accessibility and online education innovation, they have provoked concern about accentuation of inequalities and considerable concern around the issues of pedagogy, quality assurance and poor completion rates, as well as certification and recognition of learning.[87] Quality is a particular worry as MOOCs essentially involve self-study and lack the structure of other online courses.[88] Teaching methods have been criticized as outdated, because most MOOCs still rely on 'information transmission, computer-marked assignments and peer assessment'.[89] The lack of personal interactions and live discussion makes it difficult to fully respond to individual students' needs.[90]

---

[86] Yuan, L. and Powell, S. 2013. *MOOCs and Open Education: Implications for Higher Education – A White Paper*. Centre for Educational Technology, Interoperability and Standards. http://publications.cetis.ac.uk/2013/667 [Accessed February 2015].

[87] Daniel, J.S. 2012. Making Sense of MOOCs: Musings in a Maze of Myth, Paradox and Possibility. *Journal of Interactive Media in Education*. Vol. 3, No. 18. http://jime.open.ac.uk/article/view/259 [Accessed February 2015].

[88] Butcher, N. and Hoosen, S. 2014. *A Guide to Quality in Post-Traditional Online Higher Education*. Dallas, TX, Academic Partnerships. www.icde.org/filestore/News/2014_March-April/Guide2.pdf [Accessed February 2015].

[89] Bates, T. 2012. *What's right and what's wrong about Coursera-style MOOCs?* www.tonybates.ca/2012/08/05/whats-right-and-whats-wrong-about-coursera-style-moocs [Accessed February 2015].

[90] Daniel, op. cit.

Likewise, student assessment and certification is often lacking or inadequate in MOOCs. Although institutions have started to award credits for MOOCs, and novel forms of certifications such as badges are being introduced, these are still seen as an inferior form of educational outcome and an inadequate indication of the quality of learning.[91] Such criticisms may be more relevant to universities in the global North, as MOOCs may serve different needs and different constituencies in the global South.

Box 12. Towards post-traditional forms of higher education

Our usual image of a higher education institution is of a place where people go once in their lives, often between 18 and 22 years old, to move through it in a linear fashion over four years. We think of the classroom and the lecturer as the primary sources of information and the campus as the centre of learning.

However, that image is changing rapidly. The workplace is demanding skills such as communication and critical thinking that we may more easily acquire from informal learning experiences than in institutions. [...] Likewise, new methods of distance education and online learning are transforming the student experience, even on campus.

Source: Butcher, N. and Hoosen, S. 2014. *A Guide to Quality in Post-Traditional Online Higher Education*. Dallas, TX, Academic Partnerships.

Challenges to the traditional university model

One of the main challenges for higher education today is how it can respond to the massive global demand for professional qualifications while maintaining its key role in training *for* research and *through* research. The social contract that binds higher education institutions to society at large needs to be redefined in a context of increased global competition. This poses a number of fundamental questions about the future of the university model as we know it. Indeed, the landscape of higher education is being transformed by the diversification of structures and institutions, the internationalization of higher education provision, the development of MOOCs noted above, the emerging culture of assessment of the quality and relevance of learning, and growing public-private partnerships. This changing context has significant implications for financing and human resources, it questions established forms of educational governance, and it raises concerns about the principle of autonomy and academic freedoms that are the foundations of the traditional university model.

> The social contract that binds higher education institutions to society at large needs to be redefined in a context of increased global competition.

---

[91]   Bates, op. cit.

University rankings: Uses and misuses[92]

The development of university rankings reflects an important trend in the internationalization of higher education and the growing interest in the comparison of the quality of higher education institutions. While interest in university rankings has greatly increased, much criticism has also been heard from academics, students, education service providers, policy-makers and development agencies. On the positive side, rankings address the growing demand for accessible, manageably packaged and relatively simple information on the 'quality' of higher education institutions. This demand is fuelled by the need to make informed choices about universities, within a context of the massification of higher education and the fast-growing diversity of providers. For many, rankings have also encouraged transparency of information and accountability of higher education institutions. Critics, however, argue that rankings can divert universities' attention away from teaching and social responsibility towards the type of scientific research valued by indicators used for ranking exercises. There have also been concerns that by applying a limited set of criteria to world universities, and given the strong desire to feature in the top 200 universities, rankings actually encourage the homogenization of higher education institutions, making them less responsive and less relevant to their immediate contexts. The fact that rankings are also said to favour the advantage enjoyed by the 200 best-ranked institutions has important implications for equity.

---

[92]   Abstracted and adapted from Marope, P.T.M., Wells, P.J. and Hazelkorn, E. 2013. *Rankings and Accountability in Higher Education: Uses and Misuses*. Paris, UNESCO.

■ The role of educators in the knowledge society

Digital technologies do not replace teachers[93]

> The teacher should be a guide who enables learners, from early childhood throughout their learning trajectories, to develop and advance through the constantly expanding maze of knowledge.

The formidable increase in the volume of information and knowledge available requires a qualitative approach to its transmission, dissemination and acquisition, at individual and collective levels. Given the potential of information and communication technologies, the teacher should now be a guide who enables learners, from early childhood throughout their learning trajectories, to develop and advance through the constantly expanding maze of knowledge. In these circumstances, some initially predicted the teaching profession was doomed to a progressive disappearance. Such voices claimed that new digital technologies would gradually replace teachers, bringing about a broader dissemination of knowledge, improved accessibility and, above all, savings in means and resources in the face of enormously expanded access to education. We must recognize, however, that such forecasts are no longer cogent: an effective teaching profession must still be considered a priority of education policies in all countries.

Reversing the deprofessionalization of teachers

If education is to contribute to the full realization of the individual and a new model of development, teachers and other educators remain key actors. However, although dominant discourse repeatedly articulates the importance of teachers, a number of trends point to a process of deprofessionalization of teachers in both the global North and the global South. These trends include the influx of unqualified teachers, partly in response to teacher shortages, but also for financial reasons; the casualization of teachers through contract-teaching, particularly in higher education where reliance on adjuncts to meet the teaching workload is increasing; the reduced autonomy of teachers; the erosion of the quality of the teaching profession as a result of standardized testing and high-stake teacher evaluations; the encroachment, within educational institutions, of private management techniques; and gaps between the remuneration of teachers and of professionals in other sectors in many countries.

---

[93] Abstracted and adapted from Haddad, G. 2012. Teaching: A profession with a future. *Worlds of Education*. No. 159.

Box 13. Teachers highly trained and regarded in Finland

According to the Programme for International Student Assessment (PISA) of the Organisation for Economic Co-operation and Development (OECD), Finland is one of the countries with the best achievement scores in reading, mathematics and science for 15-year-olds. While this success could be attributed to many factors, it is largely due to Finland's highly trained, professional and respected teachers. In Finland, teaching is a prestigious career and the Finnish society puts trust in education and teachers. They are highly qualified (requiring at least a Master's degree for full time employment) and job selection is a rigorous process with only the best candidates chosen for teacher training. Teachers have high competence in content knowledge and pedagogy, and are autonomous and reflective academic experts.

Source: Niemi, H., Toom, A. and Kallioniemi A. (eds). 2012. *Miracle of Education: The Principles and Practices of Teaching and Learning in Finnish Schools* .Rotterdam, Sense Publishers.

We must, therefore, rethink the content and objectives of teacher education and training. Teachers need to be trained to facilitate learning, to understand diversity, to be inclusive, and to develop competencies for living together and for protecting and improving the environment. They must foster classroom environments that are respectful and secure, encourage self-esteem and autonomy, and use a wide range of pedagogical and didactical strategies. Teachers must relate productively to parents and communities. They need to work in teams with other teachers for the benefit of the school as a whole. Teachers should know their students and their families, and be able to relate teaching to their specific contexts. They should be able to choose relevant content matter and use it productively in the development of competencies. They should use technology together with other materials as instruments for learning. Teachers should be encouraged to continue learning and developing professionally.

> We also have to offer teachers more attractive, motivating and stable living and working conditions, including salaries and career prospects. This is essential if we are to avoid a dangerous loss of interest that weakens what we consider the world's most important foundational profession.

We also have to offer teachers more attractive, motivating and stable living and working conditions, including salaries and career prospects. This is essential if we are to avoid a dangerous loss of interest that weakens what we consider the world's most important foundational profession. The missions and careers of teachers must constantly be recast and reconsidered in the light of new requirements and new challenges to education in a constantly changing globalized world. To this end, teacher training at all levels – from the most general to the most specialized – must better integrate the very essence of the transdisciplinary spirit: an interdisciplinary approach that can enable our teachers and professors to lead us down the road to creativity and rationality, towards a humanism of shared progress and development, with respect for our common natural and cultural heritage.

Challenges for the academic profession

The status and working conditions of the academic profession worldwide are under strain due to both mass access and budget constraints. While the profession faces different challenges in different regions, the professoriate is confronting significant difficulties everywhere. The expansion of access to higher education has produced a tremendous need for university teachers, but qualified academics are not being produced fast enough to meet the demand. It is possible that up to half of the world's university teachers have only earned a bachelor's degree. In much of the world, half the academic staff is close to retirement. There are also too few new PhDs produced to replace those leaving the profession, since many doctoral candidates drop out early or prefer to work outside of academe because of its inadequate compensation for their work. In many Latin American countries, up to 80 per cent of teachers in higher education are employed part-time. This phenomenon undermines the quality of teaching since university teachers cannot devote their full attention to teaching, let alone to research. Moreover, in recent years, a global academic marketplace has developed: academics are internationally mobile. While better pay is a main motivating factor in explaining such flows, other factors include improved working conditions, particularly research infrastructures, as well as opportunities for advancement and academic freedom. The phenomena of 'brain drain' and of 'brain circulation', which are considered in more detail later, pose challenges to policy-making and provision in higher education.

Educators beyond the formal sector

Finally, we must recall the essential role that educators play in ensuring learning throughout life and beyond formal education systems. The importance of this role is evidenced in the growth of training programmes worldwide for educators working in a variety of non-formal and informal settings. Such educators provide learning opportunities through community centres, religious organizations, technical and vocational training centres, literacy programmes, voluntary associations, youth groups, sports and arts programmes. The value of such learning opportunities to the development and well-being of individuals and communities is considerable.

> We must recall the essential role that educators play in ensuring learning throughout life and beyond formal education systems.

3. Education policy-making in a complex world

3. Education policy-making in a complex world

Globalization is increasingly challenging the autonomy of nation-states and rendering policy-making more complex. For instance, although economic activity is increasingly globalized, political decision-making and action remain essentially at the national level. National policy-makers are thus finding it increasingly difficult to respond to and regulate the consequences of globalization for national development. The impact of the world economic crisis of 2008, for instance, or the rise in youth unemployment, including in countries of the North, are evidence of this reality. In the same way, the growing mobility of learners and workers across national borders, new patterns of brain circulation, as well as new forms of civic engagement are posing fresh challenges for national policy-making. In this section we consider examples of how this affects educational policy-making.

■ The growing gap between education and employment

Low employment growth and rising vulnerability

The intensification of economic globalization is producing patterns of low-employment growth, rising youth unemployment and vulnerable employment, affecting societies both in the global North and in the global South. Low-employment growth has recently affected parts of Europe where a new generation of young people is facing the prospect of entering employment either late or not at all. We should, however, recall that the challenges of matching skill sets acquired through education and training to labour market demand are not new.[94] We should note furthermore that although youth unemployment signals a mismatch between education, training and employment, it

---

94   See, for example: Blaug, M. 1965. The Rate of Return on Investment in Education in Great Britain. *The Manchester School*. Vol. 33.

is also linked to economic policy choices and political responsibilities. Nevertheless, current employment trends are calling into question the long-established link between formal education and employment, on the basis of which international development discourse and practice have long rationalized investment in human capital.

Growing frustration among youth

The fact that appropriate jobs are becoming scarcer is causing increasing frustration among families and young graduates around the world. Rising levels of educational attainment among youth, and workers more generally, are leading to increased competition for jobs. In many countries of the global South in particular, the entry into a constricted labour market of large numbers of young people, often the first in their communities to have benefited from expanded access to education, is exacerbating the gap between the aspirations created by formal education and the realities of scarce employment. Significant numbers of those entering formal education for the first time will no longer reap the expected benefits of educational qualifications: employment and the promise of a better future. Disillusion is growing in some segments of society and in certain countries with education as an effective vehicle for upward social mobility and greater well-being. The hope for upward social mobility spurred by the massive expansion of access to educational opportunities since the 1990s is diminishing, not only in many countries in the South, but also in the North. Young people are beginning to question the 'return on investment' of traditional 'high status' educational routes.[95]

> Disillusion is growing in some segments of society and in certain countries with education as an effective vehicle for upward social mobility and greater well-being.

Yet it is important to take a closer look and better understand the dynamics of this transition from education and training to work among youth. The prolongation of this transition period may be due to various reasons, not all related to the mismatch between skill profiles and labour market needs. Although this transition time can be seen as economically 'unproductive', for some youth it may also represent a period of important learning through social engagement, volunteering, travel, leisure, arts and other activities. Moreover, educated youth, even when not in employment, can be at the forefront of civil, social and political engagement.

Reconsidering the link between education and the fast-changing world of work

A number of responses have been proposed to address this disconnection between formal education and training and the world of work, including retraining of workers, second chance programmes and stronger partnerships with industry. We have also noted a greater focus on career-adaptive competencies. Indeed, the quickening pace

---

95   Facer, K. 2011. *Learning Futures: Education, Technology and Social Challenges*. New York, Routledge.

of technological and scientific development is making it increasingly difficult to forecast the emergence of new professions and associated skill needs. This has spurred efforts to establish more responsive education and professional skills development that include greater diversification and flexibility, allowing for the adaptation of competencies to rapidly changing needs. It implies ensuring that individuals are more resilient and can develop and apply career adaptive competencies most effectively.[96] These competencies often include more emphasis on what have been variably 'transferable skills', 'twenty-first century skills', and 'non-cognitive skills', including communication, digital literacy, problem-solving, team work and entrepreneurship.

Box 14. Strengthening employment opportunities for youth

Given the complexity of the youth employment problem, it is often noted that solutions will remain small and marginal if the critical stakeholders fail to band together with clear, comprehensive strategies and commitments. This collective approach to achieving better results and impact has been shown to work in a number of diverse industries and geographies.

In South Africa, where two out of three South Africans between the ages of 18 and 28 are unemployed, the Harambee Youth Employment Accelerator is helping a select group of low-income South African youth 'bridge' to their first jobs in the private sector. Although currently small in scale, the initiative provides a positive model for private sector engagement. Some of South Africa's largest companies in the retail, hospitality and tourism sectors are partnering to provide the job commitments. The South African Development Bank has established a Jobs Fund that provides resources, matched by private investors and employer fees, to allow Harambee to scale up its programmes.

In Costa Rica, CAMTIC, the industry association of technology companies, is implementing the Specialist programme to match vulnerable young people with needed Information Technology (IT) skills to fill a gap of several thousand unfilled jobs in the IT sector. Educational institutions, informed by IT companies like Cisco, Microsoft and others, have designed certificate-level training courses that combine soft skills, language and technical training and result in jobs that pay three to five times the country's minimum wage.

Source: Banerji, A., Lopez, V., McAuliffe, J., Rosen, A., and Salazar-Xirinachs, J.M., with Ahluwalia, P., Habib, M., and Milberg, T. 2014. An 'E.Y.E.' to the Future: Enhancing Youth Employment. *Education and Skills 2.0: New Targets and Innovative Approaches.* Geneva, World Economic Forum.

Several key questions are thus posed. How can the link between education and employment be strengthened? How can the economic and social value of education and training be enhanced in the current context? How can the relevance of education, particularly at the secondary level, be enhanced to make it more responsive to the lives of young students and to their prospects for employment? Are existing measures sufficient? Ultimately, the solution is employment creation, which implies reinforcing the

---

[96] UNESCO. 2011. *Education and Skills for Inclusive and Sustainable Development Beyond 2015.* Thematic Think Piece for the UN Task Team on the Post-2015 International Development Agenda. Paris, UNESCO.

responsibility of the state for the development of sound employment policies. Education alone cannot solve the problem of unemployment. This requires reconsidering the dominant model of economic development which would also be an opportunity to rethink the link between education and the world of work. Finally, it is important to recognize the importance of learning and relearning that continues beyond formal education and training systems. Relevant competencies are also developed through self-learning, peer-learning, work-based learning (including internships and apprenticeships), on-the-job training, or through other experiences of learning and skills development beyond formal education and training. We must therefore envisage new approaches to education and skills development that capitalize on the full potential of all learning settings.

Education alone cannot solve the problem of unemployment.

■ Recognizing and validating learning in a mobile world

Changing patterns of human mobility

Human mobility, both internationally and internally within countries, has reached the highest levels in history.[97] One in seven inhabitants in the world, or approximately one billion people, may be considered to be 'on the move' in today's world.[98] While South-North migration flows continue, South-South migration flows are growing even more rapidly and are likely to increase even faster in the future.[99] Moreover, the 'changing geography of economic growth'[100], with its consequences for employment and welfare, is encouraging an increasing number of people living in the North to relocate to the South.[101] These shifting patterns of human mobility have important consequences for education and for employment.

From brain drain to brain gain

Given global demographic trends, the majority of the world's work force is destined to be located in the South. It is estimated that 25 per cent of the world's work force, or the 'global talent pool', will by 2030 be supplied by India alone. Such patterns of brain circulation raise concerns about public funding for education and skills development, given that a significant share of this workforce migrates to live and work abroad. Estimates for 2012 put the cost of such 'human capital flight' from India at 2 billion US dollars.[102] We must note, however, that brain drain can also result in a brain gain, because migrants develop diaspora networks and serve as resources for capital and technological flows to their home countries.[103]

---

97   Rio+20, UNCSD. 2012. Migration and sustainable development. *Rio 2012 Issues Briefs*. No. 15, p. 1.
98   International Organization for Migration. 2011. *World Migration Report 2011. Communicating effectively about migration*. Geneva, International Organization for Migration.
99   UN DESA. 2011. *Urban Population, Development and the Environment*. New York, United Nations.
100   OECD. 2011. *Perspectives on Global Development 2012: Social Cohesion in a Shifting World*. Paris, OECD.
101   IOM. 2013. Migrant, Well-Being and Development. *World Migration Report 2013*. Geneva, IOM; OECD. 2013. *International Migration Outlook 2013*. Paris. OECD.
102   Winthrop, R. and Bulloch, G. 2012. *The Talent Paradox: Funding education as a global public good*. Brookings Institution. www.brookings.edu/blogs/up-front/posts/2012/11/06-funding-education-winthrop [Accessed February 2015].
103   Morgan, W. J., Appleton, S. and Sives, A. 2006. *Teacher mobility, brain drain and educational resources in the Commonwealth*. Educational Paper No. 66. London, UK Government Department for International Development.

Box 15. Reverse migration to Bangalore and Hyderabad

Bangalore and Hyderabad are considered 'worldwide leading cities' with a niche status in the global Information Technology (IT) sector. During the 1970s and 1980s, there was concern that India was losing its educated workforce to the West, particularly to the United States through a phenomenon known as 'brain drain'. More recently, evidence indicates that reverse brain drain is occurring, as U.S.-trained Indian professionals are returning to their home country in increasing numbers to take advantage of new growth and employment opportunities. Skilled, transnationally active labor forces have an impact on various sectors of the economy, on the social and physical infrastructure of Bangalore and Hyderabad, and in forging and solidifying transnational linkages between India and the United States.

Source: Chacko, E., 2007. From brain drain to brain gain: reverse migration to Bangalore and Hyderabad, India's globalizing high tech cities. *GeoJournal*, 68 (2), pp. 131-140

Increased mobility of workers and learners

In addition to increased movement of skilled labour across national borders, we see more mobility of workers across professional occupations. In response to this growing professional and geographical mobility, National Qualification Frameworks (NQFs) have been developed in some 140 countries around the world. Similarly, regional qualification frameworks, often inspired by the European Qualifications Framework (EQFs), have appeared. But the growing scale and the changing patterns of migration are making the mobility of skilled labour increasingly complex and global across all regions of the world.

Likewise, the number of globally mobile students has climbed significantly during the first decade of the twenty-first century and is expected to continue escalating. As a result, regional conventions on the recognition of studies, diplomas and degrees in higher education no longer suffice to respond to the internationalization of higher education and the growing mobility of students.

Mobility of learners, furthermore, is not confined to the circulation of students between formal educational institutions. It also includes the growing mobility of learners across formal, non-formal and informal learning spaces. This raises questions about the assessment and validation of knowledge and competencies, regardless of the multiple pathways through which they are acquired.

Growing interest in large-scale assessments of learning: Benefits and risks

> From a traditional focus on the content of education and training programmes, we are now shifting to focusing on the recognition, assessment and validation of knowledge acquired.

From a traditional focus on the content of education and training programmes, we are now shifting to focusing on the recognition, assessment and validation of knowledge acquired. Beyond the development of outcomes-based national and regional qualifications frameworks, large-scale assessments of skills levels among adults are gaining prominence, such as the Programme for the International Assessment of Adult Competencies (PIAAC) of the Organisation for Economic Co-operation and Development (OECD). Regarding learners, concern with the quality of education has spurred significant growth in the number and scope of large-scale learning assessments over the past two decades.[104] These large-scale assessments can serve as valuable tools for national accountability of public and private investment in education, particularly by monitoring the learning outcomes of those most disadvantaged by educational systems. But such assessments are also a cause for concern. They risk undermining the quality, relevance and diversity of educational experiences by encouraging teaching to the test and thus a convergence in curriculum development.[105] Policy attention tends to be focused on a narrow range of educational outcomes. The risks associated with large-scale assessments are particularly great when they are used for purposes other than informing educational policy, such as determining teacher pay or school rankings.

Towards open and flexible lifelong learning systems

Recognition and validation of knowledge and competencies acquired through multiple learning pathways are nonetheless part of a lifelong learning framework. As we have shown, societal developments are reinvigorating the relevance of education that is lifelong and life-wide. The concept is not new, but it maintains its prominence as a means of systematizing and organizing learning in a comprehensive and equitable way.[106] It places the empowerment of learners of all ages at centre stage.[107] Given the challenges of technological and scientific development, and the exponential growth in

---

104 UNESCO. 2014. *Teaching and Learning: Achieving quality for all. EFA Global Monitoring Report 2013-2014.* Paris, UNESCO.

105 For the trend toward the globalization of curricula see, for instance, Baker, D. and LeTendre, G.K. 2005. *National Differences, Global Similarities: World Culture and the Future of Schooling.* Stanford CA, Stanford University Press.
See also: IBE UNESCO. 2013. *Learning in the post-2015 education and development agenda.* Geneva, IBE UNESCO. Text available in English, French, Spanish, and Arabic

106 See, for example: UNESCO. 2014. *The Muscat Agreement.* Global Education for All Meeting. Muscat, Oman 12-14 May 2014, ED-14/EFA/ME/3 and United Nations. 2014. *Open Working Group proposal for Sustainable Development Goals.* New York, UN General Assembly.

107 UNESCO Institute for Lifelong Learning. 2010. *Annual Report 2009.* Hamburg, UNESCO Institute for Lifelong Learning.

information and knowledge that we have noted, lifelong learning is critically important to coping with new employment patterns and achieving the levels and types of competencies required by individuals and societies.

The operationalization of open and flexible lifelong learning systems depends on mechanisms for the recognition, validation and assessment of knowledge and competencies across educational and working spaces:

Societal developments are reinvigorating the relevance of education that is lifelong and life-wide.

- **Linking transparent outcomes-based qualification frameworks**

It is in this spirit that the Third International Conference on Technical Vocational Education and Training (Shanghai 2012) put forward the following recommendation: 'Support flexible pathways and the accumulation, recognition and transfer of individual learning through transparent, well-articulated outcome-based qualifications systems.'

- **Towards 'World Reference Levels' for the recognition of learning?**

The massive growth of the interregional movement of workers is motivating current feasibility studies on developing World Reference Levels for the recognition of knowledge and competencies at the global level.[108]

- **Towards an international convention for the recognition of higher education**

Beyond regional conventions for the recognition of higher education, UNESCO has recently begun exploring the possibility of elaborating an international convention for the recognition of higher education.

■ Rethinking citizenship education in a diverse and interconnected world

Emerging expressions of citizenship

Public education has always had an important social, civic and political function; it is related to national identity, the creation of a sense of shared destiny and the shaping of citizenship. The notion of citizenship refers to an individual's membership in a political community defined within a nation-state. As such, citizenship can be a contested notion, subject to interpretations, particularly in divided societies. Basic rights associated with citizenship may be denied to minority groups, including migrant groups and refugees. Today the definition of citizenship remains centred on the nation-state, but the concept and its practice is changing under the influence of globalization.[109] Transnational social and political communities, civil society and activism are expressions of emerging

---

108   Keevy, J. and Chakroun, B. 2015. *The use of level descriptors in the twenty-first century.* Paris, UNESCO.
109   Adapted from Tawil, S. 2013. Education for 'global citizenship': A framework for discussion. *ERF Working Papers,* No. 7. Paris, UNESCO.

'post-national' forms of citizenship.[110] By creating new economic, social and cultural spaces beyond nation-states, globalization is contributing to the advent of new modes of identification and mobilization beyond the limits of the national state.

Challenges for national education

The role of the state in the definition and formation of citizenship is thus being increasingly challenged by the emergence of transnational forms of citizenship. This is true even though the state remains the most important location for citizenship, both 'as a formal legal status and a normative project or an aspiration'.[111] New communication technologies and social media are an essential catalyst for this transformation, particularly among youth. Indeed, today's youth represent a formidable opportunity as they are the most educated, informed and connected generation in human history. They are increasingly engaged in alternative modes of civil, social and political activism spurred on by social media and technologies that provide them with new avenues for mobilization, collaboration and innovation. The role of formal education in civic and political socialization is challenged by the influence of the new spaces, relations and dynamics offered by digital media. Furthermore, the new digital world characterized by blogs, Facebook, Twitter and other social media requires us to rethink key notions of and distinctions between the public and the private.

> The role of formal education in civic and political socialization is challenged by the influence of the new spaces, relations and dynamics offered by digital media.

Recognition of cultural diversity and rejection of cultural chauvinism

There is growing recognition of cultural diversity, whether historically inherent to nation-states (including linguistic and cultural minorities and indigenous peoples) or resulting from migration. Migration, in particular, is contributing to greater cultural diversity within education systems, the workplace and society generally. Yet we are also witnessing a rise in cultural chauvinism and identity-based political mobilization that present serious challenges to social cohesion throughout the world. While cultural diversity is a source of enrichment, it can also give rise to conflict when social cohesion is under strain.

Fostering responsible citizenship and solidarity in a global world[112]

Education has a crucial role in promoting the knowledge we need to develop: First, a sense of shared destiny with local and national social, cultural, and political

---

[110]   Sassen, S. 2002. Towards Post-national and Denationalized Citizenship. E.F. Isin and B.S. Turner (eds), *Handbook of Citizenship Studies*, London, Sage Publications Ltd, pp. 277-291.
[111]   Ibid.
[112]   Tawil, op.cit.

environments, as well as with humanity as a whole; second, an awareness of the challenges posed to the development of communities, through an understanding of the interdependence of patterns of social, economic and environmental change at the local and global levels; and third, a commitment to engage in civic and social action based on a sense of individual responsibility towards communities, at the local, national and global levels.

- **Celebrating cultural diversity in education**

Education should celebrate cultural diversity. Enhanced diversity in education can improve the quality of education by introducing both educators and learners to the diversity of perspectives and the variety of lived worlds. The cultural dimension of education must be stressed, in the spirit of the 2001 UNESCO Universal Declaration on Cultural Diversity and the 2005 Convention on the Protection and Promotion of the Diversity of Cultural Expressions.[113]

- **Encouraging inclusive policy-making**

Increased diversity presents challenges for reaching consensus on educational policy options that most directly influence and shape identity. This aspect is perhaps most explicit in the choice of language(s) of instruction and the nature of citizenship education, including the study of history, geography, social studies and religion in multicultural societies. More inclusive processes of consultation on key policy issues are essential to constructive citizenship education in a diverse world.

■ Global governance of education and national policy-making

Emerging forms of global governance

Systems of norm-setting and regulation in the delivery of global goods such as education are not new, but they are becoming more complex. Traditionally these systems were the responsibility of national governments and inter-governmental organizations, but we are seeing increasing participation by a range of non-state actors. 'There is now a myriad of governmental and non-governmental, for profit and non-profit, actors involved in multiple – and even competing – governance arrangements at the global level.'[114] The result is a progressive shift in the locus of authority from the state to the global level where it is promoted not only

> Governance arrangements at the global level have become more complex.

---

113 Sharp, J. and Vally, R. 2009. Unequal cultures? Racial integration at a South African university *and* Stoczowski, W. 2009.UNESCO's doctrine of human diversity: a secular soteriology? *Anthropology Today*, 25 (3) June 2009, pp. 3-11.

114 NORRAG. 2014. Global governance in education and training and the politics of data scoping workshop report. www.norrag.org/en/event/archive/2014/June/16/detail/scoping-meeting-on-the-global-governance-of-education-16-17-june.html [Accessed February 2015].

by intergovernmental organizations but also increasingly by civil society organizations, corporations, foundations and think tanks. Governance arrangements at the global level have also become more complex, as illustrated by multistakeholder arrangements such as the Global Partnership for Education (GPE). The potential influence of global governance arrangements in education and skills development is arguably more controversial than in other development sectors such as health. This is because of the fundamentally political nature of national education policy and the multiple and intertwined ethical, cultural, economic, social and civic dimensions it comprises.

Accountability and associated data needs

Data are vital to governance and to accountability for the diverse stakeholders involved in and concerned by public education at both national and global levels. At the national level, it is crucial that education authorities be in a position to account for how a significant share of public expenditure (supplemented by sizeable private investment) is ensuring the right of all children, youth and adults to basic educational opportunities that lead to effective and relevant learning. Likewise, it is key that national authorities be able to account for ensuring equal opportunity for post-basic education and training. At the global level, data are increasingly standardized and quantifiable in the form of internationally-comparable statistics, indicators and composite indices, as well as large-scale assessment data, all of which are used for monitoring, benchmarking and rankings.[115] Such data are increasingly used to inform, as well as to legitimate policy-making and investment in education.

On the basis of such rationales, there has been a call for a 'data revolution' relative to the various dimensions of development.[116] Indeed, the experience of global target setting within the MDG and EFA experience since 2000 has encouraged reporting of aggregate national data, most often masking the extent of inequality and disparity within countries. If our concern is with *equity* in the provision of effective and relevant learning opportunities for all, then national targetsetting should allow for the reporting of much more disaggregated data. Data collection and use must go beyond traditional factors of discrimination such as gender and urban or rural residence, to include income and, where possible, minority status. This can be done through better use of alternative data sets such as household living standards, health or labour surveys.

Changing patterns of educational financing

As access to both basic and post-basic education expands, we have greater awareness of the pressures being placed on public financing of formal education and training systems. The resulting need is to seek more efficient use of these limited resources; to ensure greater accountability in the investment of public resources for education;

---

115 Ibid. These include PISA, PIACC, UIS and OECD statistics, and SABER.
116 United Nations. 2013. *A New Global Partnership: Eradicate poverty and transform economies for sustainable development.* The Report of the High-Level Panel of Eminent Persons on the Post-2015 Development Agenda. New York, United Nations.

and to find ways to supplement them through greater fiscal capacity, advocacy for increased official development assistance and new partnerships with non-state actors. Donors have traditionally played an important role in supplementing national public spending, particularly for basic education. It has been noted that 'Public statements of multilateral institutions suggest a strong commitment to education. In addition, surveys of developing country stakeholders in governments, civil society and the private sector show a strong demand for educational support more widely. However, despite this strong prioritization and demand, there is evidence that multilateral support for basic education is slowing compared with other sectors.'[117] The decline comes precisely at a time when some countries need it most.[118] Indeed, the share of international aid to public education remains important for many low-income countries. In nine countries, all in sub-Saharan Africa, international aid represents more than a quarter of public spending on education.[119] Moreover, the growing recognition of brain circulation across national borders is driving the call for global collective action, in particular for a funding mechanism that may supplement national public expenditure for education as a global public good.[120]

The influence of donors on national policy-making

Donors not only provide development aid to supplement much needed domestic resources, they also wield tremendous influence on education policy. This can have both positive and negative effects. For example, the Civil Society Education Fund (CSEF) and the Global Partnership for Education (GPE) have promoted the participation of civil society in Local Education Groups (LEG). This initiative enables civil society to participate in the development of educational programmes together with governments and donors and to track progress towards achieving the EFA goals.[121] However, when donors impose conditions or rules for the giving of aid, governments may be forced to change their policies accordingly.[122] The current trend of financing by results, which a number of donor agencies have adopted, may achieve their desired objectives. But it may be at variance with the policies of individual countries, and at the expense of home-grown, owned, contextually relevant and sustainable solutions. Donors should therefore support governments, local civil society and stakeholders in the development

---

[117] Pauline, R. and Steer, L. 2013. *Financing for Global Education Opportunities for Multilateral Action: A report prepared for the UN Special Envoy for Global Education for the High-level Roundtable on Learning for All.* Center for Universal Education (CUE) at Brookings Institution and UNESCO EFA GMR. It addresses issues concerning the financing of basic education (Basic Education at risk). www.brookings.edu/~/media/research/files/reports/2013/09/financing%20global%20education/basic%20 education%20financing%20final%20%20webv2.pdf [Accessed February 2015].

[118] Bokova, I. 2014. Opening Speech. *Global Education for All Meeting.* 12-14 May 2014. Muscat, Sultanate of Oman. www.unesco.org/new/fileadmin/MULTIMEDIA/HQ/ED/ED_new/pdf/UNESCO-DG.pdf [Accessed February 2015].

[119] UNESCO. 2012. *Youth and skills: Putting education to work. EFA Global Monitoring Report 2012.* Paris, UNESCO, p. 146.

[120] Winthrop, R. and Bulloch, G. 2012.

[121] GPE web site www.globalpartnership.org/civil-society-education-fund [Accessed February 2015].

[122] Moyo, D. 2009. *Dead Aid: Why Aid Is Not Working and How There Is Another Way for Africa.* London, Penguin Books.

and implementation of policies that take into account national aspirations, priorities, contexts and conditions.

Changing dynamics of international cooperation

Since the publication of the Delors Report (1996) and the adoption of the MDGs (2000), the dynamics of international aid have changed considerably. While North-South aid flows remain crucial, South-South and triangular cooperation has been playing an increasingly important role in international development. The global financial crisis and emergence of new economic powers have also contributed to changing relations between countries and creating a new international aid architecture. As countries face increasingly similar difficulties (unemployment, inequalities, climate change, etc.), there is now a call for universality and integration as essential features of the future post-2015 development agenda. Universality indeed implies that all countries will need to change their development path, each with its own approach and according to its own circumstances. This paradigm shift compels us to think in terms of shared responsibilities for a shared future.

> Since the publication of the Delors Report (1996) and the adoption of the MDGs (2000), the dynamics of international aid have changed considerably.

4. Education as a common good?

4. Education as a common good?

"By regarding education as an end in itself we recognize knowledge to be one of the ultimate values.**"**

Abul Kalam Azad, Minister of Education of India (1947-1958)

In re-visioning education in a new global context, we need to reconsider not only the purposes of education, but also how learning is *organized*. In light of the diversification of partnerships and the blurring of boundaries between public and private, we need to rethink the principles that guide educational governance and, in particular, the *normative* principle of education as a public good and how this should be understood in the changing context of society, state and market.[123]

■ The principle of education as a public good under strain

Growing call for inclusion, transparency and accountability

Individuals and communities are becoming empowered through the deepening of democracy in many countries and through the expanded access to knowledge, both through formal education and through digital technologies. This expansion is prompting a growing demand for voice in public affairs and for change in the modes of local and global governance. Popular demand is increasing for greater accountability, openness, equity and equality in public affairs. Although much of the popular demand for greater

---

123 Morgan, W. J. and White, I. 2014. Education for Global Development: Reconciling society, state, and market. *Weiterbildung*, 1, 2014, pp. 38-41.

voice is at the local or national levels, it is also increasingly transnational and addresses issues of global concern. A greater role is implied for non-state actors, be they civil society organizations or corporations, in the management of public affairs at the local, national and global levels. This holds true for education policy where both public and private sectors have a stake in the building of inclusive knowledge societies. We see such increased voice having an impact on curricula frameworks, textbooks and policies concerning affirmative action.

> Popular demand is increasing for greater accountability, openness, equity and equality in public affairs.

Growing private engagement in education

The trend towards the privatization of education is growing at all levels of provision across the world. Over the past decade, enrolment in private educational institutions has increased, particularly for primary education in lower-income countries, and for post-secondary non-tertiary education in more developed economies and in Central Asia.[124] The privatization of education may be understood as the process of transferring activities, assets, management, functions and responsibilities relating to education from the state or public institutions to private individuals and agencies.[125] In the case of school education, this process takes a variety of forms, including faith schools, low-fee private schools, foreign aid or international schools run by non-governmental organizations (NGOs), Charter, Contract and Vouchers schools, home schooling and personal tutoring, market-oriented and for-profit schools.[126] While the involvement of the private in education is not new, 'what is new about these manifestations is their *scale*, *scope*, and *penetration* into all aspects of the education endeavour.'[127]

The impact of privatization on the right to education

The privatization of education can have a positive impact for some social groups, in the form of increased availability of learning opportunities, greater parental choice and a wider range of curricula. However, it can also have negative effects resulting from insufficient or inadequate monitoring and regulation by the public authorities (schools without licences, hiring of untrained teachers and absence of quality assurance), with potential risks for social cohesion and solidarity. Of particular concern: 'Marginalised groups fail to enjoy the bulk of positive impacts and also bear the disproportionate burden of the negative impacts of privatisation.'[128] Furthermore, uncontrolled fees demanded by private providers could undermine universal access to education. More

---

124 UIS database. Time period: 2000-2011.
125 Adapted from: Right to Education Project. 2014. *Privatisation of Education: Global Trends of Human Rights Impacts*. London, Right to Education Project.
126 Patrinos, H.A. et al. 2009. *The Role and Impact of Public-Private Partnership in Education*. Washington, DC, World Bank. Lewis L., and Patrinos H.A. 2012. *Impact Evaluation of Private Sector Participation in Education*. London, CfBT Education Trust. Right to Education Project. 2014. *Privatisation of Education: Global Trends of Human Rights Impacts*. London, Right to Education Project.
127 Macpherson, I., Robertson, S. and Walford, G. 2014. *Education, Privatization and Social Justice: case studies from Africa, South Asia and South East Asia*. Oxford, Symposium Books.
128 The Right to Education Project. 2014. op. cit.

generally, this could have a negative impact on the enjoyment of the right to a good quality education and on the realization of equal educational opportunities.

Supplemental private tutoring, or 'shadow education', which represents one specific dimension of the privatization of education, is also growing worldwide.[129] Often a symptom of badly functioning school systems,[130] private tutoring, much like other manifestations of private education, can have both positive and negative effects for learners and their teachers. On one hand, teaching can be tailored to the needs of slower learners and teachers can supplement their school salaries. On the other hand, fees for private tutoring may represent a sizeable share of household income, particularly among the poor, and can therefore create inequalities in learning opportunities. And the fact that some teachers may put more effort into private tutoring and neglect their regular duties can adversely affect the quality of teaching and learning at school.[131] The growth of shadow education, the financial resources mobilized by individuals and families, and the concerns regarding possible teacher misconduct and corruption are leading some ministries of education to attempt to regulate the phenomenon.[132]

Box 16. Private tutoring damages the educational chances of the poor in Egypt[133]

In Egypt, private tuition is a significant part of household education spending, averaging 47% in rural areas and 40% in urban areas. The amount spent annually on private tutoring was reported to be US$2.4 billion, equivalent to 27% of government spending on education in 2011.

The investment is viewed as worth the financial strain for families that can pay. However, not everyone can afford it: children from rich households are almost twice as likely to receive private tuition. Children whose families cannot afford private tutoring suffer the consequences of a poor quality formal education system in which teachers are more likely to spend their energy and resources on private tutoring than in the classroom.

An important reason for widespread private tuition is that the social status of teachers in Egypt has declined in recent decades as the government began hiring less qualified teachers to meet the demand of growing public education. School-leavers often become teachers not by choice but as a last resort. The undervaluing of teachers in Egyptian society has made teaching one of the lowest-paid government jobs. Teachers thus turn to private tutoring to supplement their salaries.

Source: UNESCO. 2014. *Teaching and Learning: Achieving quality for all. EFA Global Monitoring Report 2013-2014.* Paris, UNESCO.

---

129 Bray, M. 2009. *Confronting the shadow education system. What government policies for what private tutoring?* Paris, UNESCO-IIEP.
130 UNESCO. 2014. *Teaching and Learning: Achieving quality for all. EFA Global Monitoring Report 2013-2014.* Paris, UNESCO.
131 Bray, M. and Kuo, O. 2014. Regulating Private Tutoring for Public Good. Policy options for supplementary education in Asia. *CERC Monograph Series in Comparative and International Education and Development.* No. 10. Hong Kong, Comparative Education Research Center and UNESCO Bangkok Office.
132 Ibid.
133 UNESCO. 2014. *Teaching and Learning: Achieving quality for all. EFA Global Monitoring Report 2013-2014.* Paris, UNESCO. [Based on the following sources: Central Agency for Public Mobilization and Statistics (2013); Elbadawy et al. (2007); Hartmann (2007); UNESCO (2012a).]

The reproduction and possible exacerbation of inequalities of learning opportunities resulting from privatization in all its forms raises important questions about the notion of education as a public good and about the role of the state in ensuring the right to education.

Recontextualizing the right to education

International development discourse often refers to education as both a human right and a public good. The principle of education as a fundamental human right that enables the realization of other human rights is grounded in international normative frameworks.[134] It denotes a role for the state in ensuring the respect, fulfilment and the protection of the right to education. Beyond its role in the provision of education, the state must act as a *guarantor* of the right to education.

> The reproduction and possible exacerbation of inequalities of learning opportunities resulting from privatization raises important questions about the role of the state in ensuring the right to education.

Box 17. Respecting, fulfilling and protecting the right to education

46. The right to education, like all human rights, imposes three types or levels of obligations on States parties: the obligations to respect, protect and fulfil. In turn, the obligation to fulfil incorporates both an obligation to facilitate and an obligation to provide.

47. The obligation to respect requires States parties to avoid measures that hinder or prevent the enjoyment of the right to education. The obligation to protect requires States parties to take measures that prevent third parties from interfering with the enjoyment of the right to education. The obligation to fulfil (facilitate) requires States to take positive measures that enable and assist individuals and communities to enjoy the right to education. Finally, States parties have an obligation to fulfil (provide) the right to education. As a general rule, States parties are obliged to fulfil (provide) a specific right in the Covenant when an individual or group is unable, for reasons beyond their control, to realize the right themselves by the means at their disposal. However, the extent of this obligation is always subject to the text of the Covenant.

Source: UN Committee on Economic, Social and Cultural Rights (CESCR). 1999. *General Comment No. 13: The Right to Education (Art. 13 of the Covenant)*, 8 December 1999, E/C.12/1999/10 (46/47), available at: www.refworld.org/docid/4538838c22.html [Accessed 6 March 2015]

Despite the specific legal obligations related to the various provisions of the right to education, much of the discussion on the right to education has, until recently, focused on schooling, and perhaps even more narrowly on primary schooling. The notion of basic

---

[134] See, in particular, the 1948 Universal Declaration of Human Rights (Art. 26), the 1966 International Covenant on the Economic, Social and Cultural Rights (Art. 13), and the 1989 Convention on the Rights of the Child (Art. 28).

education adopted in 1990 at the World Education Forum (WEF) in Jomtien, Thailand, was broad. It comprised both the basic learning tools, such as literacy and numeracy, and context-responsive basic knowledge, skills and values. From the perspective of formal education, basic education is most often equated with compulsory schooling. The vast majority of countries worldwide have national legislation that defines periods of schooling as compulsory. Seen from this angle, the principle of the right to *basic* education is uncontested, as is the role of the state in protecting this principle and ensuring equal opportunity.

However, while these principles are relatively uncontested at the level of basic education, there is no general agreement about their applicability at post-basic levels of education.[135] The expansion of access to basic schooling has also resulted in a growing demand for secondary and tertiary education and in an increasing concern for vocational skills development, particularly in the context of growing youth unemployment, and with a continuous process of qualification and requalification. Given this growing demand for post-basic education and for lifelong learning, how are the principles of the right to education to be understood and applied? How does it differ from the right to basic (compulsory) schooling in terms of entitlements of rights-claimants and responsibilities of duty-bearers? What are the responsibilities and obligations of the state at post-compulsory levels of education, whether upper secondary education, higher education, and technical and vocational education at secondary and tertiary levels? How can responsibility be shared while preserving the principles of non-discrimination and equality of opportunities in access to post-basic levels of education and training?

Blurring of boundaries between public and private

Education is often referred to as a public good in international education discourse. The United Nations Special Rapporteur on the Right to Education has underlined the importance of preserving the social interest in education, while promoting the concept of education as a public good.[136] However, the primary responsibility of states in the provision of public education is increasingly being contested with calls for reduced public spending and greater involvement of non-state actors. The multiplication of stakeholders, including civil society organizations, private enterprise and foundations, as well as the diversification of sources of financing, is blurring the boundaries between public and private education. It is no longer clear what the notion of 'public' means in the new global context of learning, characterized by a greater diversification of stakeholders, by the weakening capacity of many nation-states to determine public policies, and by emerging forms of global governance. The nature and degree of private engagement in educational provision is blurring the boundaries between public and private education. This is evident, for example, in the growing reliance of public higher

---

135 Morgan, W. J. and White, I. 2014. The value of higher education: public or private good? *Weiterbildung*, 6, 2014, pp. 38-41.
136 Singh, K. 2014. *Report of the Special Rapporteur on the right to education.* United Nations. A/69/402, 24 September 2014. http://ap.ohchr.org/documents/dpage_e.aspx?si=A/69/402 [Accessed February 2015].

education institutions on private funding; the growth of both for-profit and nonprofit institutions; and the introduction of business methods in the operation of higher education institutions. Emerging forms of the private – where both basic and post-basic education are opening up increasingly to profit-making and trade and to agenda-setting by private, commercial interests – are changing the nature of education from a public to private (consumer) good.[137] The rapidly changing relationship of society, state and market is creating a dilemma. How can the core principle of education as a public good be protected in the new global context in which learning takes place?

> How can the core principle of education as a public good be protected in the new global context?

■ Education and knowledge as global common goods

The limits of public good theory

Public good theory has a long tradition and has its foundation in market economics.[138] In the 1950s, public goods were defined as those goods 'which all enjoy in common in the sense that each individual's consumption of such a good leads to no subtractions from any other individual's consumption of that good'.[139] The transfer of an essentially economic notion to the field of education has always been somewhat problematic. Public goods are considered to be more directly linked to public and state policy. The term *public* often leads to a common misunderstanding that 'public goods' are goods *provided by the public*.[140] On the other hand, *common goods* have been defined as those goods that, irrespective of any public or private origin, are characterized by a binding destination and necessary for the realization of the fundamental rights of all people.[141]

From this perspective the concept of the 'common good' may prove to be a constructive alternative. The common good may be defined as 'constituted by goods that humans share intrinsically in common and that they communicate to each other, such as values, civic virtues and a sense of justice.'[142] It is 'a solidaristic association of persons that is more than the good of individuals in the aggregate'. It is the good of being a community

---

137 Macpherson, Robertson and Walford, op.cit., p. 9.
138 Menashy, F. 2009. Education as a global public good: the applicability and implications of a framework. *Globalisation, Societies and Education*, Vol. 7, No. 3, pp. 307-320.
139 Samuelson, P. A. 1954. The Pure Theory of Public Expenditure, *The Review of Economics and Statistics*, Vol. 36, No. 4, pp. 387-389.
140 Adapted from Zhang, E. 2010. *Community, the Common Good, and Public Healthcare – Confucianism and its relevance to contemporary China*. Department of Religion and Philosophy, Hong Kong Baptist University.
141 Adapted from Marella, M.R. 2012. *Oltre il pubblico e il privato: per un diritto dei beni comuni*. Verona, Ombre Corte.
142 Deneulin, S., and Townsend, N. 2007. Public Goods, Global Public Goods and the Common Good. *International Journal of Social Economics*, Vol. 34 (1-2), pp. 19-36.

– 'the good realized in the mutual relationships in and through which human beings achieve their well-being'.[143] The common good is therefore inherent to the relationships that exist among the members of a society tied together in a collective endeavour. Goods of this kind are therefore inherently common in their 'production' as well as in their benefits.[144] From this perspective, the notion of common good allows us to go beyond the limits of the concept of 'public good' in at least three ways:

1. The notion of common good goes beyond the instrumental concept of the public good in which human well-being is framed by individualistic socio-economic theory. From a 'common good' perspective, it is not only the 'good life' of individuals that matters, but also the goodness of the life that humans hold in common.[145] It cannot be a personal or parochial good.[146] It is important to emphasize that the recent shift from 'education' to 'learning' in international discourse signals a potential neglect of the collective dimensions and the purpose of education as a social endeavour. This is true both for the broader social outcomes expected of education, and for how educational opportunities are organized. The notion of education as a 'common good' reaffirms the collective dimension of education as a shared social endeavour (shared responsibility and commitment to solidarity).

> The notion of common good goes beyond the instrumental concept of the public good in which human well-being is framed by individualistic socio-economic theory.

2. What is meant by the common good can only be defined with regard to the diversity of contexts and conceptions of well-being and common life. Diverse communities will therefore have different understandings of the specific context of the common good.[147] Given the diverse cultural interpretations of what constitutes a common good, public policy needs to recognize and nurture this diversity of contexts, worldviews and knowledge systems, while respecting fundamental rights, if it is not to undermine human well-being.[148]

3. The concept emphasizes the *participatory* process, which is a common good in itself. The shared action is intrinsic, as well as instrumental, to the good itself, with benefits derived also in the course of shared action.[149] Education as a common good therefore necessitates an inclusive process of public policy formulation and implementation with due accountability. Placing common goods beyond the public or private dichotomy implies conceiving and aspiring towards new forms and institutions of participatory democracy. These would need to go beyond

---

143   Cahill cited in: Deneulin and Townsend, ibid.
144   Adapted from: Deneulin and Townsend, ibid.
145   Deneulin and Townsend, ibid.
146   Holster, K. 2003. The Common Good and Public Education. *Educational Theory*, 53(3), 347-361.
147   Zhang, op.cit.
148   Deneulin, and Townsend, op.cit.
149   Adapted from Deneulin and Townsend, ibid.

current policies of privatization without returning to traditional modes of public management.[150]

Recognizing education and knowledge as global common goods

Education is the deliberate process of acquiring knowledge and developing the competencies to apply that knowledge in relevant situations. The development and use of knowledge are the ultimate purposes of education, guided by principles of the type of society to which we aspire. If education is seen as this deliberate and organized process of learning, then any discussion about it can no longer be focused solely on the process of acquiring (and validating) knowledge. We must consider not only how knowledge is acquired and validated, but also how access to it is often controlled and, therefore, how access to it can be made commonly available.

Box 18. Knowledge creation, control, acquisition, validation and use

Knowledge can be understood broadly as encompassing information, understanding, skills, values and attitudes. Competencies refer to the ability to *use* such knowledge in given situations. Discussions about education (or learning) are habitually concerned with the intentional process of *acquiring* knowledge and developing the ability (competencies) to use them. Educational efforts are also increasingly concerned with the validation of knowledge acquired.

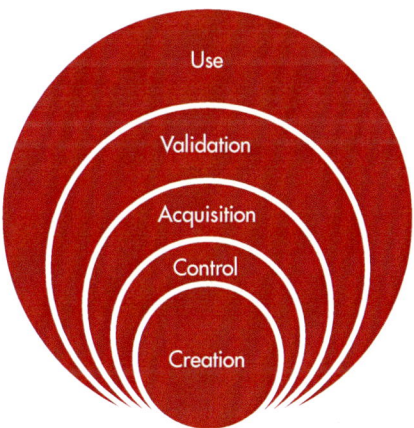

However, discussions about education and learning in today's changing world need to go beyond the process of acquiring, validating and using knowledge: They must also address the fundamental issues of the *creation* and *control* of knowledge.

Source: Authors

---

150   Marella, op. cit.

Knowledge is the common heritage of humanity. Knowledge, like education, must therefore be considered a global common good. If knowledge is considered only a global *public* good[151], access to it is often restricted.[152] The current trend towards the privatization of knowledge production, reproduction and dissemination is a cause for serious concern. The knowledge commons is gradually being privatized through law and, more specifically, through the Intellectual Property Rights regime, which dominates knowledge production. The progressive privatization of the production and reproduction of knowledge is evident in the work of universities, think tanks, consultancy firms and publishing. As a result, much of the knowledge we consider a public good, and which we believe belongs to the knowledge commons, is actually being privatized. This is disturbing, especially when it comes to the ecological and medicinal knowledge of indigenous communities that is being appropriated by global corporations. Some resistance to this trend is emerging among indigenous peoples. It is also producing counter movements of sharing in the digital world such as the Linux software that gives users the freedom to run, copy, distribute, study, modify and improve the original product.[153]

> Education and knowledge should be considered global common goods. The creation of knowledge, its control, acquisition, validation, and use, are common to all people as a *collective social endeavour*.

Given the central concern for sustainable development in an increasingly interdependent world, education and knowledge should thus be considered global common goods. This means that the creation of knowledge, its control, acquisition, validation, and use, are common to all people as a *collective social endeavour*. The governance of education can no longer be separated from the governance of knowledge.

Protecting foundational principles

It is important to underline that current international education discourse carries with it a potential for undermining foundational principles that have guided international and national education policy and practice. Indeed, the current international education discourse couched in terms of *learning* is essentially centred on the *results* of educational processes and tends to neglect the *process* of learning. In focusing on results, it is essentially referring to *learning achievement*[154]: that is, to the knowledge

151 Kaul, I., le Goulven, K. et al. (eds) 1999. *Global Public Goods. International Cooperation in the 21st Century,* New York, Oxford University Press.
152 Stiglitz, J. 1999. *Knowledge as a global public good.* In Kaul, I., le Goulven K. et al. (eds), ibid., pp. 308-325. See also UNDP. 1999. *Human Development Report.* New York, Oxford University Press.
153 www.linuxfoundation.org [Accessed February 2015].
154 'Learning achievement refers to the actual skills, attitudes, values and level of knowledge acquired by the individual; it implies some measurement or demonstration that learning has occurred.' World Conference on Education for All. 1990. *Meeting Basic Learning Needs: A vision for the 1990s. Background Documents.* New York, Inter-Agency Commission for the WCEFA.

and skills that can most easily be *measured*. It tends thereby to neglect a much wider spectrum of results of learning, involving knowledge, skills, values and attitudes that can be considered important for individual and societal development, on the grounds that they cannot be measured (easily). Furthermore, learning is seen as an *individual* process of skill acquisition, and little attention is paid to questions of the purpose of education and the organization of learning opportunities as a *collective social endeavour*. This discourse thus potentially undermines the principle of education as a *common good*.

Roles and responsibilities in the regulation of common goods

Inspired by the values of solidarity and social justice grounded in our common humanity, the principle of knowledge and education as global common goods has implications for the roles and responsibilities of diverse stakeholders in the collective quest for sustainable and inclusive human and social development.

- **Enhancing the role of civil society and other partners**

It is vital, in the current context, to promote a more significant and more explicit role for civil society in education. The current trends towards the commodification of public education should be countered by stronger partnerships with community associations and non-profit organizations. Indeed, education – in its multiple functions – is not only a responsibility of government, but of society as a whole. Good governance in the education sector requires multiple government-civil society partnerships and national education policy should be the result of wide social consultation and national consensus.

Innovative mechanisms for financing development by corporate sectors and foundations have been experimented with in recent years, particularly in education. This experimentation has also contributed to the expansion of effective and innovative partnerships among all development partners – countries, private sector, civil society, academia, citizens – to leverage external partners' expertise, capacities and resources. Many examples exist of successful partnerships that have helped achieve tremendous results, even with traditionally considered public goods such as education.

Private business can also play a key role by investing in education beyond immediate employment needs as part of its corporate social responsibility. In India, for instance, the state is encouraging private companies to invest 2 per cent of annual turnover in this way. Corporate social responsibility funds could be used to contribute to the social and educational needs of underprivileged communities. Legislation, which provides tax benefits to the businesses concerned, may be required to raise these additional resources.

- **Strengthening the role of the state in the regulation of common goods**

In the current context of economic globalization and market liberalization, the state must maintain its function of ensuring access to and regulating common goods, in education particularly. Education must not be ceded entirely to the market, as it constitutes the first link in the chain of equality of opportunity. From this perspective, the state has two obligations:

> Education must not be ceded entirely to the market, as it constitutes the first link in the chain of equality of opportunity.

1. To reform public education and to professionalize it, including through countering corruption within the sector using clear procedures making it more accountable to society at large.

2. To monitor and regulate the involvement of the private sector in education. Monitoring should by no means be administrative and bureaucratic – it should not be a policing function. The state's monitoring function should ensure the application of standards adopted by education professionals working in both public and private sectors, as well as of international normative frameworks.

- **Strengthening the role of intergovernmental agencies in the regulation of global common goods**

The international community has a responsibility for the governance of global common goods. Global good governance is an issue for the United Nations system and for other international organizations, which must strengthen their cooperation in both policy and practice. Beyond their technical functions, United Nations agencies have a role in international norm-setting to guide the governance of global common goods such as knowledge, education, and tangible and intangible cultural heritage. In this regard, it is appropriate to recall two domains in which UNESCO has taken a lead coordinating and inspirational role: the Education for All movement and the elaboration of the normative aims of education.[155]

---

155 Bray, M. and Kwo, O. 2014. Regulating Private Tutoring for Public Good Policy Options for Supplementary Education in Asia. *CERC Monograph Series in Comparative and International Education and Development,* No. 10. Comparative Education Research Center, University of Hong Kong.

■ Considerations for the way forward

This discussion, inspired by a central concern for sustainable human and social development, outlines the trends, tensions and contradictions in global social transformation, as well as the new knowledge horizons offered. It highlights the importance of exploring alternative approaches to human well-being and the diversity of worldviews and knowledge systems, and the need to sustain them. It reaffirms a humanistic education, which calls for an integrated approach based on renewed ethical and moral foundations. It points towards an educational process that is inclusive and does not simply reproduce inequalities: a process in which fairness and accountability are ensured. It emphasizes that the role of teachers and other educators remains central to fostering critical thinking and independent judgement, instead of unreflective conformity.

The text examines issues of educational policy-making in a complex world. One, we need to recognize and to respond to the gap between formal education and employment. Two, we must face the challenge of recognizing and validating learning in a world of increasing mobility across borders, professional occupations and learning spaces. Three, we must rethink citizenship education, balancing respect for plurality with universal values and concern for common humanity. Finally, we consider the complexities of national policymaking in education, together with potential forms of global governance. As we signal these issues, many questions remain unanswered.

The discussion also explores the need to recontextualize foundational principles for the governance of education, particularly the right to education and the principle of education as a public good. It proposes that greater attention be paid in education policy to knowledge, and to the ways in which it is created, acquired, validated and used. It proposes that considering education and knowledge as global common goods could be a useful approach to reconciling the purpose and organization of learning as a collective societal endeavour in a changing world.

> There is a need to recontextualize foundational principles for the governance of education, particularly the right to education and the principle of education as a public good.

In considering the way forward and as a call for dialogue, a number of questions are proposed for further debate:

> While the four pillars of learning – to know, to do, to be and to live together – are even more relevant today, they are threatened by both globalization and the resurgence of identity politics. How can they be strengthened and renewed?

How can education better respond to the challenges of achieving economic, social and environmental sustainability? How can this humanistic approach be realized through educational policies and practices?

How can a plurality of worldviews be reconciled through a humanistic approach to education? What are the threats and the opportunities of globalization for national policy and decision-making in education?

How should education be financed? What are the implications for teacher education, training, development and support? What are the implications for education of the distinction between the concepts of private good, public good and common good?

UNESCO, as the specialized United Nations agency for education, together with the related areas of science, culture, and communications, should strengthen its role as a 'laboratory of ideas' monitoring global development trends and the implications for learning. This would be in accordance with UNESCO's educational mandate and its role as an intellectual agency and think tank.[156] Because it is no longer effective to develop policy in isolation, diverse stakeholders with their multiple perspectives should be brought together to share research findings and to articulate normative principles in the guidance of policy.

> Diverse stakeholders should be brought together to articulate normative principles in the guidance of policy.

It is also worth noting that UNESCO is exceptional in the United Nations system in having global networks of National Commissions, UNESCO Chairs and specialized institutes. These networks could be used more intensively as a means of re-evaluating the purpose and assessing the practice of education on a regular basis, as circumstances and needs change. This should be achieved through a permanent observatory mechanism that reviews and reports on development trends and their implications for education.

Humanity has entered a new phase in its history with increasingly rapid developments in science and technology. These have both utopian and dystopian possibilities. For us to benefit in an emancipatory, just and sustainable way, we must understand and manage the opportunities and the risks. Making this possible should be the fundamental purpose of education and learning in the twenty-first century. It should also be the basic task of UNESCO, as a global laboratory of ideas, to enhance our understanding of such possibilities with the aim of sustaining humanity and its common well-being. This publication is intended as a contribution to stimulating the debate.

---

156 Elfert, M. 2015. UNESCO, the Faure Report, the Delors Report, and the Political Utopia of Lifelong Learning. *European Journal of Education.* Vol. 50, No. 1, pp. 88-100.